ROCK · LIVES

THE ULTIMATE STORY

THE ARTIST FORMERLY KNOWN AS
Prince

THE ARTIST FORMERLY KNOWN AS

Prince

STEVEN ROSEN

Design: Slatter-Anderson
Printed through: World Print, Hong Kong
Cover photograph: Pictorial Press Ltd
Photographs: Neal Preston, Redferns, Pictorial Press Ltd

Published by Castle Communications plc, A29 Barwell Business Park, Leatherhead Road,
Chessington Surrey, KT9 2NY.

Copyright: Castle Communications plc 1995

While the publishers have made every reasonable effort to trace the copyright owners
for any or all of the photographs in this book, there may be some omission of credits for
which we apologise.

ISBN: 1 860740 456

He's the man of a thousand faces and each one of them is a mask, a mystery to be unravelled and interpreted. So enmeshed is he in this cloak of invisibility, that in 1993, 7 June (his birthday), he laid to rest the name 'Prince', and adopted a derivative of the male/female symbol as a substitute. Some people called him 'the artist formerly known as Prince', others addressed him simply as Symbol or Icon, and still some followers jocularly referred to him as 'Symbol Man', 'What's-His-Symbol' and 'The Glyph'.

Needless to say, he's an artist representing a load of questions and very few answers. Anybody working for or around him calls him 'The Boss', a title given to another high profile artist, but in this case, one which carries serious weight. In the few interviews he's been obliged to give, Prince (as this book will refer to him for the moment), has been labelled a 'genius', a 'perfectionist' and just plain 'weird'.

The man, born on 7 June, 1958 in Minneapolis, Minnesota, is indeed all these personality types, and it is this yin/yang, good/bad, sort of schizo-androgynous-revolutionary mantle he wears so well which accounts for his extraordinarily unique style of music. It is a sound both urban and rural, sensuous and sadistic, music for the eleventh hour, a combination of R&B, pop and dance.
To appreciate better what it is Prince does, it's helpful to journey back in time about 38 years or so to Mount Sinai Hospital in Minneapolis. Prince

Roger Nelson has just been born on this seventh day of June to John L. Nelson, a pianist, and Mattie Shaw, a singer. Prince, actually named after his father's band the Prince Rogers Band, has inherited the music gene from both mom and dad. Mattie sang in her husband's group until marriage and the burdens of motherhood made it impossible for her to leave the house.

Tika Evene (later spelt Tyka), a sister, would be born two years later; Prince, however, would have other siblings. His parents eventually divorced and re-married divorcees, and he ended up with one half-brother and two step-siblings through his father's new union.

Prince, in various interviews, has talked about his parents and it is apparent, very early on, how important music was to become.

'My mom's the wild side of me, she's like that all the time. My dad's real serene. It takes the music to get him going. My father and me, we're the same. He's a little sick – just like I am!'
This sickness would result in John's departure from the family – Prince is seven years old. Two years later Mattie would re-marry. Prince is focused on the experience in a candid interview.

'I was living at home with my mother and Tyka. Then my step-dad arrived when I was nine, and I disliked him immediately because he dealt with a lot of materialistic things. He would bring us a lot of presents all the time, rather than sit down and talk with us and give us companionship.'

Prince was 12 when he first ran away from home; arguments in the household and increasing tension with his stepfather were the main reasons. Many times he ended up at his Aunt Lorna's, a half-sister who had the same father as Prince. Seclusion and music – two constants which would forever be a part of his life.

'He would spend hour after hour shut up in his room,' remembers Lorna Nelson, 'teaching himself to play the piano. He was always shut and very quiet and liked his music a lot, but he had a hard time at school and at home. He was always bullied at school. Every day the bigger kids would wait for him. They used to jeer at him because he was so short and had a black-Italian background. All the misery made him even more of a loner. He knows what it's like to be hurt.'

This derision would account in large part for his insolent and even rude behaviour to others. Years later, when his star had finally risen, the musician would constantly hire and fire musicians, bodyguards, publicity firms and all the other spokes necessary to make his particular wheel spin.

Needless to say, Prince did quite well in school music programmes and excelled in music theory, guitar class and stage band. He set his sights early and even went so far as to take courses in song copyrighting and recording. He found solace in the sounds to soothe the savage beast.

'I realised that music could express what you were feeling,' he explained in *Prince: The Documentary*. 'And it started coming out in my songs – loneliness and poverty and sex. My stepbrother Duane always had the girls around him and stuff like that. I think I must have been on a jealous trip because I got out of sports. I wasn't bad at basketball, but my brother was better and he wouldn't let me forget it. I just wanted to do something else... something they couldn't do.'

Music became this alternative activity. Working even harder on the piano, he started figuring out the themes to such popular television hits of the time as *Batman*, *The Man From U.N.C.L.E.* and *Dragnet*. For the most part, though, Minneapolis in the early seventies was essentially isolated musically and did

Main picture: **Prince and Dez Dickerson in an early shot. Dez was a mainstay during the early part of Prince's rise. Dickerson is picking on a Les Paul.**

Inset picture: **A rare shot from early in Prince's development. Here he plays a Fender bass, an instrument he controls with as much dexterity as a six–string.**

not have anywhere near the input of cities like New York and Los Angeles. There were a few acts such as the Castaways ('Liar Liar') and the Trashmen ('Surfin' Bird') who did put the city on the map for a brief moment. During this same period, folk artists such as Bob Dylan and Koerner, Ray & Glover, the latter a white folk and blues ensemble, were attracted to this same clime.

In 1972, Prince moved in with André Anderson, a friend from junior high school. The pair began jamming in the Anderson's basement and by age 14 both of them had mastered several instruments including guitar, keyboards, bass and drums. Chuck Orr, owner of a local music store, testified to this alliance.

'André and Prince were great friends and they both just like to come in and play. I don't pretend to be a great authority but I recognise talent and, oh, God, could Prince play! He definitely had it. He could darn near do anything he wanted to.'

Two years later, in 1974, these two formed a band called Grand Central, sometimes referred to as Grand Central Corporation. An early formation of the group included Prince on guitar, André on bass, André's sister Linda on keyboards, and two percussionists named Terry Jackson and William

Main picture(opposite): **Prince, spectacles on, putting his Telly through the motions. Note the keyboard array in background.**

Over leaf: **Prince at keyboard during the *Purple Rain* tour. The synth appears to be some sort of electric piano (probably a Yamaha).**

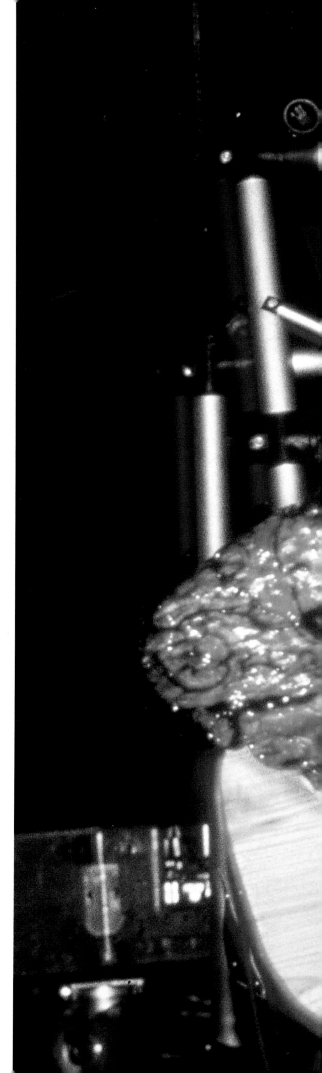

Daugherty. Charles 'Chazz' Smith played drums. In a later line-up, Daugherty's cousin Morris Day – who would eventually play in the Time – was part of the group.

They played mainly small local gigs: battle of the band contests, dances, hotel parties and YMCA festivities. Known primarily as an instrumental group, Grand Central began showcasing Prince on vocals as their reputation grew, covering songs by Larry Graham, Carole King, Grover Washington, and the Ohio Players. It was around this time that Prince began writing his own material but like Sisyphus, this was a heavy stone to roll.

'It was all Top 40 stuff. The audiences didn't want to know the songs I was writing for the group,' Prince explained. 'They'd just cover their faces, largely because of the lyrics. I remember I had this song called 'Machine' that was about this girl that reminded me of a machine. It was very explicit about her parts. People seemed to find it very hard to take. There was quite a lot of Sly Stone stuff we used to do. I really liked it when he'd have a hit because it would give us an excuse to play them.

'Listening to the radio in Minneapolis really turned me off a lot of things that were supposedly going on. If they did pick up on something, they'd just play it to death, and you'd end up totally disliking it. So I missed out on a lot of groups. When I started doing my own records, I really didn't want to listen to anybody because I figured I should disregard what anybody else might be doing. Though I suppose subconsciously I might have been influenced just by the mood that was going on around me.'

Much of that atmosphere was coloured by KQRS, Minneapolis' main progressive rock radio station. Its staples were the likes of the Allman Brothers, Santana, Hall & Oates, Grand Funk Railroad, and an especially stormy guitar player by the name of Jimi Hendrix.

In Prince's music it's easy to hear and pick out his influences: there is the melding of Sly and the Family Stone's fusion and funk, the tight and soulfully orchestrated grooves of James Brown, the Latin and lyrically orientated lines of guitarist Carlos Santana, and the more experimental and mind expanding licks of Jimi Hendrix.

'Hendrix plays different guitar than I do. If they (audiences) really listened to my stuff, they'd hear more of a Santana influence than Jimi Hendrix. Hendrix played more blues; Santana played prettier. You can't compare people, you really can't, unless someone is blatantly trying to rip somebody off.'

Main picture (opposite): The *Purple Rain* tour.
Inset picture (above): Singing his little heart out. This mic has a cord so the photo is probably a little older (he didn't go wireless until later).

Over leaf: Prince live with the New Power Generation. Second guitarist in shot, playing a Gibson, appears to be Miko Weaver.

Technicalities

1991, the Record Plant in Los Angeles. Prince has, by this time, written and recorded well over a dozen albums and established himself as an artiste of incontrovertible merit, stature and commercial clout. The bulk of his work takes place at Paisley Park, his privately owned recording complex back in Minneapolis, his main base of operations. But when he does venture outside those doors, he inevitably ends up at the Record Plant, one of the three or four premier facilities in Los Angeles – and for that matter the entire country – because he is comfortable there. And this is no small point of contention.

As has already been mentioned, he is that turbulent hybrid of introvert and extrovert, someone who deals with people in a cold-shoulder and semi-mechanical fashion, at the same time an entity consumed with the process of creation and disturbed when his ideas and visions and commands are not realised in a swift and efficient manner. This is all a reflection of those adolescent years when the family unit was constantly shifting and he had to continually defend himself as a musician and a person. He was always being compared to siblings who excelled in certain areas and, measured against them, he often fell short of expectations. Hence, the almost wordless fashion in which he dealt with people (many times he'd communicate with an exasperated shrug or perplexed grimace), and the insulated barrier he built around himself.

In this time lapse scenario, the Prince persona takes on true dimension and definition and instant appreciation of what was, in all probability, a gradual metamorphosis. This narrative will go back and fill in this approximate 17 year gap. But by creating this instantaneous, verbal time tunnel, there is an immediate appreciation and grasp of what these years of woodshedding, head banging, and internal and external pressures created.

So, it is 1991, Los Angeles, and Prince has taken up residence at the Record Plant, a state-of-the-art complex which recently celebrated its 25th anniversary ('25 Years of Hits' is the media buzzword). Kyle Bess is a staff engineer at the Plant and has been so employed for many years. Somehow, some way, he was assigned to Prince, and his insights and experiences provide a wonderful picture of the man as a musician, obviously, and also as an individual dealing with problems and situations on a day-to-day basis.

Bess, who has worked with everyone from Van Halen to David Foster, is a technician with estimable skills, yet at the same time, he is a working man who must deal with the whims, quirks and sometimes impossible demands of his clients. He recalls for this book his first meeting with Prince.

'It started in the middle of 1991 and I don't think he'd ever really worked at the Record Plant before. He had booked time there and since I was one of their main engineers, they wanted to make sure they put me on the session with him. That's when Mike Koppelman from Paisley Park was engineering for him. We got everything set up that first day and... I

don't usually get too nervous when I'm working with people but I was a little tense working with him the first time. I'd never even seen him perform before or anything in my life. So he walks in the control room and the first thing he does is he says "hi" to Mike and he looks at me and he's

Main picture (opposite): **Prince with Telecaster. The instrument was a perfect complement to his funk/rock style, allowing him to create a blacker tone – more treble, more high end – and at the same time, a rockier and edgier texture. His influences he wore on his sleeve, players such as Hendrix and Santana, but he was quick to say: 'You can't compare people, you really can't unless someone is blatantly trying to rip somebody off.'**

1991, the Record Plant in Los Angeles. Prince has, by this time, written and recorded well over a dozen albums and established himself as an artiste of incontrovertible merit, stature and commercial clout. The bulk of his work takes place at Paisley Park, his privately owned recording complex back in Minneapolis, his main base of operations. But when he does venture outside those doors, he inevitably ends up at the Record Plant, one of the three or four premier facilities in Los Angeles – and for that matter the entire country – because he is comfortable there. And this is no small point of contention.

As has already been mentioned, he is that turbulent hybrid of introvert and extrovert, someone who deals with people in a cold-shoulder and semi-mechanical fashion, at the same time an entity consumed with the process of creation and disturbed when his ideas and visions and commands are not realised in a swift and efficient manner. This is all a reflection of those adolescent years when the family unit was constantly shifting and he had to continually defend himself as a musician and a person. He was always being compared to siblings who excelled in certain areas and, measured against them, he often fell short of expectations. Hence, the almost wordless fashion in which he dealt with people (many times he'd communicate with an exasperated shrug or perplexed grimace), and the insulated barrier he built around himself.

In this time lapse scenario, the Prince persona takes on true dimension and definition and instant appreciation of what was, in all probability, a gradual metamorphosis. This narrative will go back and fill in this approximate 17 year gap. But by creating this instantaneous, verbal time tunnel, there is an immediate appreciation and grasp of

what these years of woodshedding, head banging, and internal and external pressures created. So, it is 1991, Los Angeles, and Prince has taken up residence at the Record Plant, a state-of-the-art complex which recently celebrated its 25th anniversary ('25 Years of Hits' is the media buzzword). Kyle Bess is a staff engineer at the Plant and has been so employed for many years. Somehow, some way, he was assigned to Prince, and his insights and experiences provide a wonderful picture of the man as a musician, obviously, and also as an individual dealing with problems and situations on a day-to-day basis.

Bess, who has worked with everyone from Van Halen to David Foster, is a technician with estimable skills, yet at the same time, he is a working man who must deal with the whims, quirks and sometimes impossible demands of his clients. He recalls for this book his first meeting with Prince.

'It started in the middle of 1991 and I don't think he'd ever really worked at the Record Plant before. He had booked time there and since I was one of their main engineers, they wanted to make sure they put me on the session with him. That's when Mike Koppelman from Paisley Park was engineering for him. We got everything set up that first day and... I

don't usually get too nervous when I'm working with people but I was a little tense working with him the first time. I'd never even seen him perform before or anything in my life. So he walks in the control room and the first thing he does is he says "hi" to Mike and he looks at me and he's

Main picture (opposite): **Prince with Telecaster. The instrument was a perfect complement to his funk/rock style, allowing him to create a blacker tone – more treble, more high end – and at the same time, a rockier and edgier texture. His influences he wore on his sleeve, players such as Hendrix and Santana, but he was quick to say: 'You can't compare people, you really can't unless someone is blatantly trying to rip somebody off.'**

like, "Uh, I'm okay right now, I'll call you when I need you." He didn't say hello or anything, just, "I'm okay right now, I'll call you when I need you." So I left the room and just hung out at the front desk. And basically he stayed in the room for the entire duration of the booking, which was about five or six hours.

'And then they (not Prince himself) came and got me because he needed to make a cassette of what he was working on and then he left.

'For *three* months he didn't say my name; he didn't acknowledge me except when he needed something. I mean he wouldn't say, "Kyle". But I heard that he does that with everybody. I guess if you're arrogant or have an attitude it would bother you, but I didn't care. I had a job to do and I was working with him and it was like "whatever". And everybody would say, "Don't take it personally, that's the way he is."

'And then one day he started calling me by name and I started getting more and more involved. He kept coming back and I kept working on the session and it just went from there to what it is now – I basically do his whole set-up. I engineer for him and he has engineers from Paisley Park, and basically when he comes out (to Los Angeles), there's an engineer from Paisley Park and me.'

Bess has become one of those spokes, an important

Main picture:
A shot taken during the
***Lovesexy* tour, 1988.**

one, and the credo he's adopted is: 'Whatever it takes to get the job done.' And this is another intriguing wrinkle in the Prince line of demand – working meticulously and aware of every note transferred to tape, he *will* make do with whatever equipment is available and not adopt the guise of prima donna if a certain piece of gear is not on hand. Again, this may harken back to those earlier Grand Central days when money was a luxury and you banged on any keyboard and strummed on any electric guitar which was in your economic grasp. But he does have an array of electronics he feels comfortable with and Bess (along with some information provided by *Guitar World*) enlightens us.

Stipulating that it would 'vary from time to time' as regards guitar choices, Bess noted that many times Prince would come with an array of instruments he brought with him from Paisley Park, and on other sessions Bess would round up guitars on his own. The main travel pieces were the so-called 'Cloud' guitars, custom-made for The Boss. Designated as 'C-1, C-2 and C-3' there are only about 20 in the world. C-1 was the elite of this series and the one Prince tended to turn to most frequently. This

Main picture (opposite): This also appears to be a shot during the *Lovesexy* tour which was his largest stage production to date.

Over leaf: Telecaster in hand, he goes through the moves before venturing back to the mic. His ability to play guitar, intricate parts, and then move gracefully back to the vocal end, is astonishing. Few artists are capable of pulling this off.

particular commodity was originally white, then painted yellow (the same guitar he's playing in most of the MTV videos), and finally finished in blue.

In typical Boss understatement, 'he walked in the room, saw this blue guitar sitting in the stand, picked it up, played it for a second, handed it back to me to put in the stand, and that was it.'

Besides the cloud guitar(s), Prince would turn to a Hohner version of the Fender Telecaster, the latter an instrument he's strapped on many times. He has a fondness for maple – the Cloud – and Fender and Hohner are all made of this type of wood. Maple has always been known as a wood to produce that crystally, twangy, high-end sort of tone and from very early on The Boss was enamoured with its sonic properties.

The Hohner was brought to prominence during the *Purple Rain* period and was the guitar used on 'When Doves Cry'.

'I know he liked Telecasters but when he picks something else up and it works, he plays it,' Bess surmises about this Hohner choice. 'The Hohner wasn't exactly the greatest sounding guitar in the world and I had a lot of problems with it in the studio as far as hums and buzzes. But he liked it and we used it a lot in the studio.'

Prince is known to abuse his instruments, that is, punish them during his live routine. After a certain point, guitars were no longer shipped out from Paisley Park when he came to L.A. and Kyle Bess was made responsible for rounding up a suitable collection. The Record Plant engineer would turn to friend Paul Jameson, called 'Jamo' by friends; funnily enough, Paul was known mainly for the renting of drums and not guitars. But he also deals in guitars and basses and it was to this person Bess usually turned.

Jameson had a Fender Precision bass, foam green colour, which Prince liked, and a black Takamine acoustic The Boss would always rent.

'I would always have to get the Takamine, which was an electric/acoustic, and this P-bass. And some sort of hollow-body, whether it be a (Gibson) ES335 or an Epiphone. He always had to have a hollow-body guitar and usually a Telly. And that was enough tools for him right there. It was funny

because sometimes he would use the hollow-body for a lot of things. Obviously, when he had his own guitars he would use the Hohner for more funky stuff and use the cloud guitar for more rock and roll stuff.

'I would rent a lot of guitars, more than I needed, and I went through a lot of guitars. Whatever I noticed he wanted to use all the time, I would just lose the others, because I was trying to save him money plus it made my life easier because it was that many less guitars I had to tune. Jamo brought me a Rickenbacker 12-string one time and after dealing with that, I would take it out and hide it. I said, "Come get it, Jamo." It was too much, I had too many other things to do. And if I didn't tune the 12-string and it was sitting there, he'd go, "Hand me the Rickenbacker." I don't understand his sort of psychic sense or whatever, but the one thing you didn't do, or the one thing you didn't check or the one thing you didn't test, you'd get caught.'

And what would happen if he strummed an out of tune guitar?

'He'd pick up the guitar and say, "Did you *ever*, like, tune this guitar?" or "This guitar feels like you just ate a Milky Way and were playing it." I'm not a guitar tech and it's frustrating because I get it to where I think it's in tune and I would have like a little amp or something there and would spend as much time as I could tweaking it. We don't know if he's going to do guitars that day, you don't know what he's going to do. So it's kinda like you have to be ready to do whatever he wants. I've seen him get really irritated about guitars being out of tune, but

Pictures : **Prince's grace, character and musicianship was not lost on the press: 'Prince teams with hooks that echo everone from the Temptations to Jimi Hendrix to Todd Rungren... The simplicity of Prince's words, hooks and rhythms are pure pop, with a trace more sophistication, he could become a solo Bee Gees of the libido.' (Rolling Stone)**

that was before the whole guitar, technical thing ended up in my lap. An engineer who no longer works with him was supposed to tune the guitars. One day he picks up the guitar and I guess it must have fallen out of the stand because it was really out of tune, and Prince says, "Do you guys tune these guitars?" And the engineer goes, "Periodically." And Prince says, "What's periodically? Is that one time a day? Once a month?" And then he just chewed the
guy out.

'But I can't really blame him because he does give you an adequate amount of time to get ready for him. The tough thing is you don't know if you're going to start at one in the afternoon or you don't know if he's going to walk in at three or four in the morning. And you kinda have to keep the studio vibe set up that whole amount of time. We're all on beepers but we prefer not to wait at home for him to call us because he might be at Fountain and La Brea (five minutes from the studio's location at 1032 Sycamore Avenue in Hollywood) and he'll say, "Okay, let's go to the studio now." That doesn't give you enough time to get down there, tune up the guitars, check all the gear and make sure everything works.

'So each day we try and gauge it. If he's been going in at one each afternoon, we'd go in around that time and get set up. Sometimes we would go in at two or three (in the afternoon), do our checks, make sure everything works, and wait. Hang out and wait.'

One of the reasons for this inconstancy in scheduling is not due entirely to caprice. Prince's record company, Warner Bros. is in Los Angeles and many times he'd have meetings and other business

to attend to. Video shoots were often located in Hollywood. Not to mention owning a club and home in the area. 'Plus the night life is a lot more active here than in Minneapolis,' Bess is quick to point out. At any given moment, he might be tied up in a meeting, hanging out at one of his Glam Slam clubs or tying up any one of a thousand loose ends.

'His bodyguards have called and said, "We're on our way" at four in the afternoon and we see him at 3:30 in the morning. So you take it with a grain of salt but you'd *better* be ready when he gets there.'

So, when he would eventually arrive, he'd strap on the cloud, Hohner, acoustic or hollow-body of some sort. He's also been known to pick on a Taylor or Guild acoustic and has from time to time shouldered a Gibson non-electric.

Another guitar which has since become a sort of trademark is the symbol or 'love' guitar. Composed of high grade maple, it features 22 frets (the original symbol has 24) and a Telecaster-styled bridge (versus the Tune-O-Matic assembly on the prototype). The neck shape is a combination Les Paul and 'Cloud' guitar feel.

The Boss would normally plug into a Soldano Caswell preamp for pristine sounds or a rackmount 100-watt Soldano head for dirt. Bess, in attempting to simplify both his life and that of the player's, experimented with a Marshall, one of the newer hot-rodded Mesa Boogies, but ultimately wound up using an Edward Van Halen signature Peavey 5150.

'Basically because it had channel switching from clean to dirty, I got a nice, good dirty guitar sound and it was easy for me to get a dirty guitar sound. And he never complained about it so... I stuck with it.'

Again, Prince was a man of few words, and he would never verbalise exactly what it was he was searching for. It all came down to a simple gesture – if he played it, the sound was acceptable.

In order to give more substance to his sound and to realise a more varied guitar attack,

Prince did make use of both a rackmount display and floor-based pedalboard. The guitar signal, initially, passes through a series of Boss stomp boxes, inexpensive but teeming with personality and texture (Hendrix, too, utilised low-priced units and this is one of the reasons why Prince and the late left-hander were compared to each other).

This pedalboard sports from left to right a metal zone (the most recent addition), a vibrato, a digital delay, an octaver, a flanger, and a turbo distortion. Another crucial piece of the puzzle is any English customised Colorsound wah (the Colorsound distortion box was a major part of Jeff Beck's sound during the Rod Stewart days).

'This is the same board he'd use in the clubs. When he was in the studio, the guitar would go through the Boss pedals before it would go through the rack. It doesn't make any sense but that's what he wants. (Because these pedals tend to be inexpensively made, they are subject to RF signals and a host of other unwanted sounds.) He likes those Boss pedals, and the other thing which no one can find anyway and something he's really fond of was the Colorsound wah-wah pedal. That's his wah-wah sound. And then again, there have been times when they didn't ship me the Colorsound or I couldn't find one, and I needed a wah-wah pedal and didn't have the time to call a rental company at ten at night. So I borrowed a wah-wah pedal from Nile Rogers in the next room, a Cry Baby. I'd fly out of the session and run into Nile's room and say, "I need a wah-wah pedal," and he said I could borrow this. And that was adequate for his needs. It's better to have some wah-wah pedal than no wah-wah pedal.'

After the guitar ran through the pedalboard, it entered a rack of outboard gear which, according to Bess, had been 'gutted and changed around so many times'. Every guitar tech, relying on their own favourite pieces, would mix and match so this column of gear was forever being rearranged. But it mainly consists of the two Soldano pieces – the Caswell for clean and the 100-watt top for dirt. Either amp may be brought into the chain via two Uptown Flash rack mixers in conjunction with any one of a number of effects. Again, these come and go but the mainstays tend to be an Alesis Quadraverb (mainly used for reverb), a Roland GP-16 (for pitchbend effects), and two customised Zoom 9030s, which are multi-textured and utilised for any number of sounds. In addition, there is a Roland VCA expression pedal assigned to the GP-16 giving him the ability to control pitch changes in real time. Some of these customised Zoom programs he has dubbed 'Twin Reverb' and 'Pillow Talk'. There is an eight-switch Roland pedalboard with which he may select programs from the Zooms and/or GP-16. The pedalboard works as a team mate with a Digital Music Corp. MXC-8 MIDI Switcher.

'There are no rules. A lot of times in the studio, I just may go direct to the console via the Boss pedalboard. Sometimes I would run the distortion sounds through a Leslie cabinet; sometimes I would run it through the Peavey 5150. A lot of times I would use the Zoom box. Sometimes it was determined because we had such a limited amount of time and we were so busy, I hadn't had time to set the guitar rig up yet. We didn't have the guitar rig set up so we didn't use it, we just used the Zoom. You know what I mean? There was no rhyme or reason.

'The thing is, I think the idea that he has is to just get some sort of sound he's happy with. Maybe he's really picky but he doesn't seem to be that way to me. He's picky about it if it hums and buzzes – he's not too fond of that. But then again, who is? But as long as it's something he can work with, he's fine. He's never really complained about what guitars I've had in there; if I had a choice, he may have a preference. I mean, I used to bring my own guitar, a '71 Telly, and I don't even know if he knows it's mine; it's just in the room. I like it because it's my guitar and I know what it's capable of doing, and I know the ins and outs of it. So that makes my life a little easier, because sometimes Jamo would fail me

in the Telly department.

Cabinets, more critical in a live setting than in a recording situation, played out in this fashion: the power stage of the 100 watt Solando head ran four cabinets – two on stage for Prince's own monitoring demands and another two off stage placed in a pit. These were miked, one out of phase, one in phase. The preamps also daisy-chained two Mesa Boogie Strategy 500 stereo power amps. One cab was assigned for each channel. The cabinets themselves were Marshall slants housing vintage Celestion 30 watt speakers for the sparkle and Peavey 5150s for the crunch. For additional control, the clean signal was also direct-injected into Paragon house mixing consoles via Countryman D.I. boxes.

This system also embodies a crown power amplifier used to drive auxiliary on-stage cabs for larger and more intricate live stage set-ups. A combination of dbx, Rocktron Hush and Guitar Silencer units acted as white noise eliminators. Prince, because he is so mobile, running, jumping and James Browning it every moment, packed a Sony wireless rig for larger houses and a Samson box for more club-sized venues.

The Record Plant is fitted out like a gear-head's dream (see appendix). With such an astonishing array of gear available to him, Prince still was not impressed with buzzers and bells. Facade meant nothing. There was no singular piece of gear to which he regularly turned, but rather he used everything in a sort of Princely pot-pourri.

'No, there was nothing he used all the time,' reaffirmed Bess. 'If he just had a selection (of

effects) up there, and he was just playing at the board, he could push the "send" button and if he liked the way it sounded he would leave it on, and if he didn't he would turn it off. That's basically what we did there.

'I guess the weirdest thing about him was you had to understand how he worked, and you had to do the gig and obviously had to do it *right*. But there was no, "Ummm, Prince, I'm going to change the guitar strings on the Telly... What kind of strings do you want?" Do you know what I mean? You don't ask those questions; you just know, you know the answers. And it does take a while to find out what he likes and dislikes.'

As Kyle Bess learned – both instinctively and musically – what made The Boss feel more at ease, he was slowly drawn into the inner circle. During those apprentice months at the Plant, Bess was forced to leave the studio whenever Prince cut vocals (no one is *ever* present – in the same way Jimmy Page vacates everybody when cutting guitar solos – during the recording of vocals). At a point, however, the engineer was allowed to stay.

'Everybody is in the control room; it was in the last two years when he really got comfortable with me, it didn't matter if I was in or out of the room. Sometimes he'd go, "You guys can go hang out now." For all I knew, he may have been watching CNN (television) in there. I don't know what he was doing – maybe he was writing lyrics or maybe the man just wanted privacy. So we'd just walk out of the room and when he needed us, he'd call us back in.

'And then sometimes it was like we *wanted* to be out of the room because we had been trapped in there for eight hours losing our minds but we couldn't get out of there.'

Prince recorded for the first time at Moon Sound Studios in Minneapolis in 1976. SSL boards and $2500 per day rooms (approximate cost of the Record Plant's Studio I) are still but dreampuffs in the distance. This facility, owned by Chris Moon, is a demo-quality three-track room renting out for $25 per hour. Moon approached Prince and band (Grand Central had changed names to Champagne) about collaborating; the studio owner fancied himself a lyricist and he was instantly struck by Prince's musicality. Moon, in another Prince biography, described the situation.

'I pulled Prince aside and said, "Look, I've got this idea I want to talk to you about. Why don't we get together, combine our resources? I'll teach you how to record, everything I know. I'll produce a demo for you. If it goes somewhere, great. If it doesn't, we both learn from the process. I don't want a contract with you; all I want is that you credit my name on the songs you end up using." There wasn't a long oratory response, just a head nod and that was the beginning of the agreement.

This pact resulted in a 50/50 split of any monies made on a collaboration. In exchange, Prince received free studio time. The other members of Champagne were against the idea, and the musician cut them loose. This wouldn't be the last time he'd sever connections with band members.

On 7 June, 1976, his 18th birthday, he graduated from Central High School and continued his work in Moon's studios. Much of his intense cramming was done here, learning how to record and laying down all instruments himself. Here again, we see the isolation and solitude. Prince actually played on some of Moon's low budget jingles and commercials and even recorded with local singer Sue Ann

Carwell. But most important was Prince's own composing chops; he wrote, among others, 'Machine', 'Aces', 'Make It Through The Storm', 'Soft And Wet', 'My Love Is Forever' and 'Leaving New York'. Two of these, 'My Love Is Forever' and 'Soft And Wet' would appear two years later on his first album (*For You*).

After this rigorous internship which lasted through the summer, Prince eventually cut his first real demo with producer David Rivkin at Sound 80 studios. Rivkin had previously worked with (the now late) Gram Parsons. This was also an important period insomuch as Prince began his serious work with synthesisers and from this the 'Minneapolis' sound as it would be called, took seed. He displayed this texture on a three-song demo including 'Soft And Wet', 'Make It Through The Night' and 'Baby' (this last cut would also be on the *For You* album).

Early in 1977, Prince began working once again with André Anderson (name changed to Cymone) for New York musician/producer Pepé Willie. This New Yorker had formed a band called 94 East (a highway linking Minneapolis to sister city, St. Paul) and Prince and André became studio musicians on the project. This album was later released as *Minneapolis Genius – The Historic 1977 Recordings*. This venture eventually fell apart, but not before the boy wonder had a chance to record several more of his songs: 'I Feel For You', which turned up on *Prince*, his second album for Warner Bros. and 'Do Me, Baby', which would appear on the *Controversy* record. ('Do Me, Baby' began as a collaboration and when Prince released it four years later, as his own, Cymone was terribly offended.)

While Prince was engaged in this studio work, his demo was being shopped in Los Angeles. RSO and

Picture (opposite):
A very early shot.
Short hair.

ABC gave him a thumbs down, but CBS/Columbia, Warner Bros. and A&M all expressed interest. On 25 June, 1977 he indeed signed with Warner Bros. Records for an undisclosed six-figure amount – one of the largest ever presented to a new artist.

In the autumn of 1977, Prince began working on his debut album at the Record Plant in Sausalito, California (a picturesque studio located across the bay from San Francisco and owned in its entirety by Warner Bros.). One of the stipulations of Prince's contract was that he be allowed to produce himself (once again, this fencing off stance), but the label insisted on an outside person. Earth, Wind & Fire's Maurice White was contacted, but a lack of time forced him to decline. Eventually, Tommy Vicari, a producer/engineer who had worked with such luminaries as Santana, Billy Preston and Gino Vanelli took on the job. Even someone with credentials such as these did not cut muster with the singer. They banged heads constantly and this in-fighting would consume five months of studio time before *For You* was finally released. Prince lays it out in *A Documentary*.

'The relationship between me and the executive producer (Vicari) they assigned me was horrifying. He was really just an engineer – he was well-versed in short-cuts but I didn't want to take any. That was why it took five months to make.'

Prince, even at this early stage, was meticulous in approach: 12-hour days were not uncommon. He did bring in Patrice Rushen, a synthesiser programmer extraordinaire, to assist in arranging.

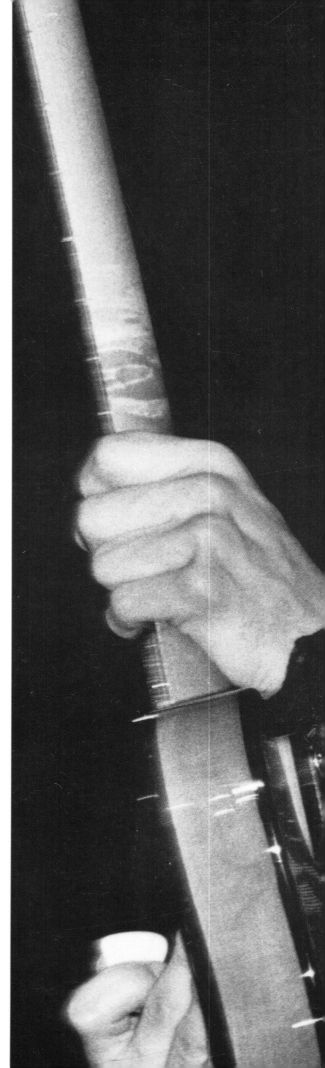

Picture (opposite):
In the arms of the guitar gods.
Again, he wrestles with
the Telecaster.

Over leaf:
In a playful mood, working
the crowd.

'I was a physical wreck when I finished the record. I didn't really feel like recording for 80 per cent of the record. But I did it anyway because by the time I had gotten close to (spending) $100,000, it was like, you were going to have to do something great. So, by that time, I didn't want to make any mistakes.'

Main picture (opposite):
Getting cozy with a vocal.

Inset picture (above):
Sweaty, in profile, he is still a commanding figure.

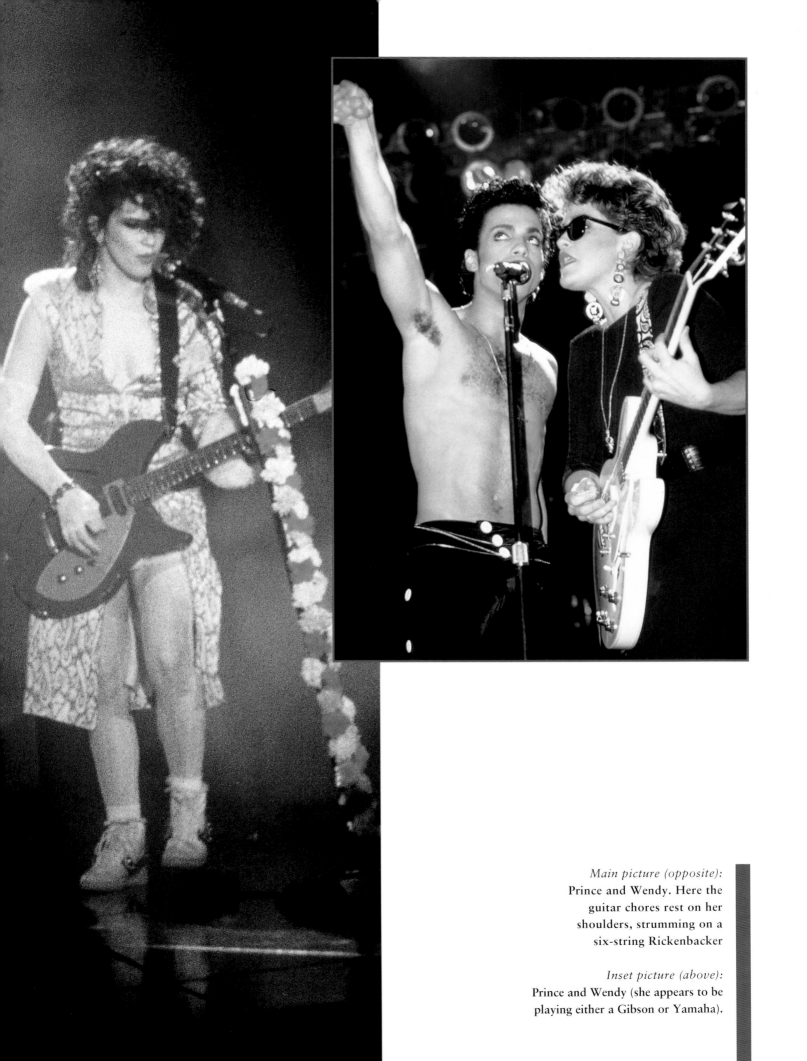

Main picture (opposite):
Prince and Wendy. Here the guitar chores rest on her shoulders, strumming on a six-string Rickenbacker

Inset picture (above):
Prince and Wendy (she appears to be playing either a Gibson or Yamaha).

This debut, released on 7 April, 1978, was the progenitor of a style being bandied about as the 'Minneapolis' sound: stacked synth parts creating a horn/brass ensemble section flying over tightly orchestrated funk grooves. And Prince, who would constantly be bending genders and definitions, icing everything with his electric guitar and waif-like falsetto vocals.

'Soft And Wet' b/w 'So Blue' was the first single release and a perfect example of this Minneapolis-styled music. It was coincidentally released on his 20th birthday and sold nearly 350,000 copies in America to reach Number 12 on the black chart but barely broke into the Top 100 – at 92 – on the pop scale. The record was essentially dominated by these layers of synths and his almost cruelly-affected high-end vocals, though on a track like 'I'm Yours' you do have a hint of what a guitar technician he would someday become.

'I wanted to make a different sounding record,' he reported to another writer. 'We originally planned to use horns, but it's really hard to sound different if you use the same instruments. By not using horns, I could make an album that would sound different right away. So I created a different kind of horn section by multitracking a synthesiser and some guitar lines. I got hip to Polymoogs when I was working at Studio 80. I liked them a lot then. I was trying to get away from using the conventional sound of pianos and clavinets as the main keyboards.'

Main picture (opposite): **Prince changing it up as he sits behind a keyboard. Steve Morse, a writer from the *Boston Globe*, saw his constant changing in this way: 'He really was the complete–entertainer, swooping into a falsetto like Smoke Robinson, slapping out boogie woogie piano chords like Little Richard, hopping back to play brain ripping guitar solos and then often sliding across the stage, tipping the microphone over and as if by magic, catching it just as it was about to fall.'**
Inset picture (above): **Dueting with Wendy Melvoin. That's Miko Weaver in left background.**

Notwithstanding his prowess as a guitarist, he is a masterful keyboard player and much of his music is centred around the ivories. We have broken the time barrier in order to land ourselves circa 1992. We're at The Record Plant. The Boss has taken up residence. What is that old chestnut? 'The more things change, the more they stay the same.' Well, Prince is still noodling with keyboards – albeit models infinitely more sophisticated and malleable than those he worked with on the early records but, at the bottom line, still tools nonetheless. We have shifted our time focus yet again in order to provide a more immediate picture of Prince as player, a bird's eye view of the Plant, if you will.

'I've never seen him labour over anything, not a keyboard part or a guitar part,' emphasises Bess. 'Probably like anybody else, if you start thinking about it then you might toy with it until you get it to work. But with him, there wasn't much labouring over anything; he made everything look too easy.

'There's no box or anything you can go and buy at Guitar Center that's gonna make you Prince. There's only one Prince. The guy can play drums, he'll kill you on bass, he'll kill you on keys and piano. He's a genius, a phenomenal musician. Whether the critics like his albums or not, his musical ability is sick, it's ridiculous what the guy can do.

'I've been in the room and been in a bad mood and he'll play something... Even after all these years and in all this time (working with him), he'll blow my mind. He'll lay a groove down when he's working on a new song and just start jamming – for no reason but just because he likes to play. He'll be playing the guitar with one hand and the keyboard with the other hand. He's not doing it to show off, he's not showing off in front of me – it's just that he's getting into it.'

One new wrinkle present here in the nineties and not a part of those early records, is his employment of a programmer. For several years Airiq Anest was used in this fashion (on the *Prince And The N.P.G.* album he is listed under 'additional programming' and 'assistant engineers'), and he would provide the princely one with drum sequences, rhythmic textures, sequenced bass lines and such. Anest is no longer Prince's programmer, his services having been discontinued.

Describes Bess, 'Prince would say "Hey, hook me up with this kind of groove" or "Put down this drum pattern for me". Airiq would do it and he (Prince) would come in and would either like it or not like it. If the groove was kind of cool, then he would build upon that. Sometimes tapes would come from Minnesota (Paisley Park) that had like basic tracks on them (drums, figured bass, scratch guitars), and then he would do a lot of overdubs on them. It was just endless.'

Because Prince's output of material was so prodigious, it was necessary to incorporate additional gear in order to allow all the mixing of this material to be accomplished in a swifter manner. Simply put, Prince was kickin' it so hard virtually 24-hours a day, that the normal process of mixdown was not fast or efficient enough.

Bess, without trying to be intentionally vague, was not exactly sure which albums/cuts he was involved in. He knows he was part of 'The Most Beautiful Girl In The World', the *Come* LP, the Carmen Elektra LP, the Tevin Campbell project, *Diamonds And Pearls*, the 'Symbol' stuff, and various songs

Main picture (opposite): This is a mid–80s shot with The Boss in skin–tight–white regalia. He sports a fuller afro here though he would change his coiffure with virtually every album release.

Over leaf: (left) This shot was taken around the release of *Parade*, the soundtrack to Under the Cherry Moon (about 1986).
(right) Prince with 'Cloud' guitar. The posture suggests he may be playing the instrument with his teeth. Note bandage on first finger of right hand.

Pictures (opposite): Circa 1986 with the Revolution. One writer noted this tour as being, 'So slick, so professional – choreography doesn't seem an apt enough word.'

for outside artists. Many times he had the New Power Generation band with him but many times he would come out from Minneapolis on his own. HE would be working on a song and when Bess inquired about the title, he would cryptically respond in a non-verbal manner. That is, he wouldn't say a word. So the engineer logged the cut as 'Thursday: groove' or 'New groove' or 'Sexy groove'. He would manufacture a name and ultimately it would evolve into a flesh and tones piece of music. He may leave the Record Plant, return to Minnesota, work on it there and watch it become a '7' or 'Diamonds And Pearls'. Prince would be labouring over a chord sequence, and Bess would leave the room for six hours, only to return and hear the piece mutated into some unrecognisable entity.

As was touched on before, no one was ever present when Mr. Nelson cut vocals. 'I don't know when he decided to do that or how long he's been doing that,' queries Bess, but basically, he would set up a microphone in the control booth which would actually extend over the board itself. But before we venture into his extreme seas of music making, we should travel back to where there are no programmers, no computers, not even a band.

Prince has already hired his new band – Cymone, née André Anderson (bass); Z, née Bobby Rivkin (drums); Dez Dickerson (guitar); and twin keyboardists Gayle Chapman and Matt Fink – and now performs as a solo artist with backing group. This chameleon is changing colours...

It is now October 19, 1979 and his second album modestly named after himself, is a deliberate effort – deliberately commercial.

'The second album was pretty contrived,' he admits in another conversation. 'I had put myself in the hole with the first record because I spent a lot of money to make it. I wanted to remedy that with the second album. I wanted a "hit" album. It was for

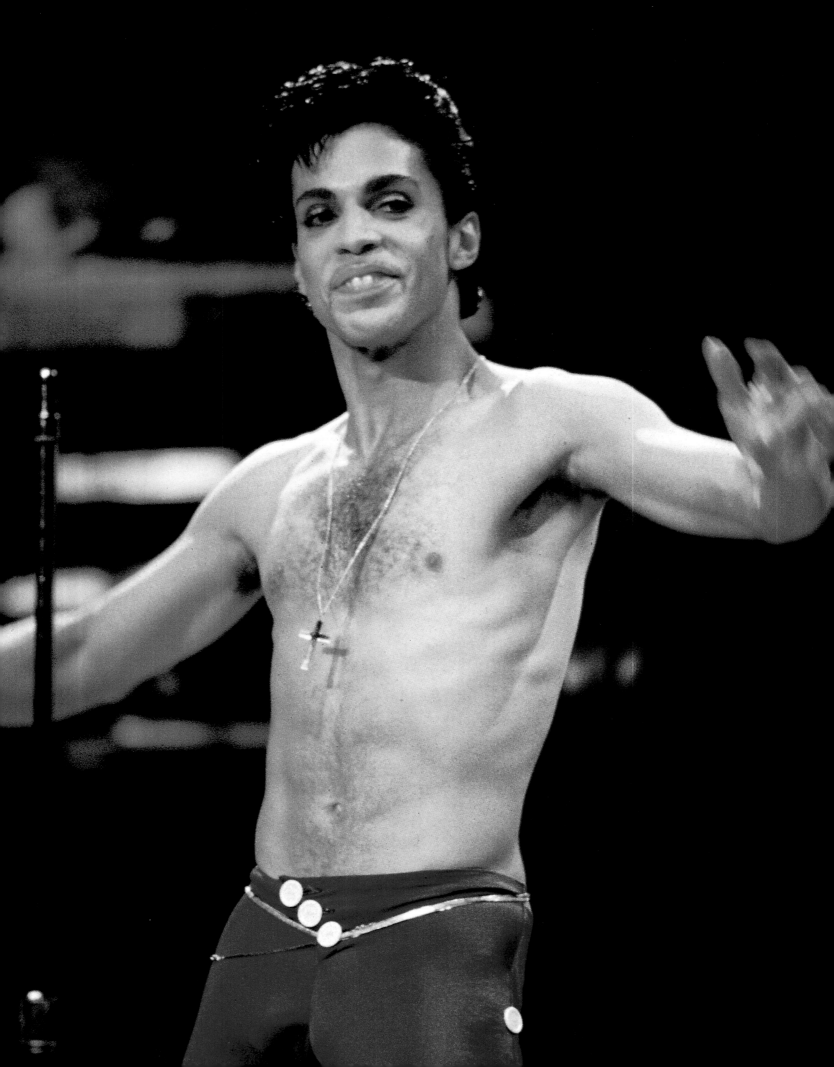

the radio rather than for me, but it got a lot of people interested in my music.'

Playing a Les Paul Jr. during this recording, he did realise a hit in the single 'I Wanna Be Your Lover', released about one-and-a-half months before the album. It made it to Number 1 on the black chart and Number 11 on the national chart in the U.S.; the album, his second for Warner Bros., found its way to Number 22 on the Billboard pop and LP chart. Though this cut featured mainly synths, tracks like 'Bambi' and 'Why You Wanna Treat Me So Bad' were centred around huge electric guitar riffs and once again offered up influences like Santana and Hendrix.

Beyond the music is the image as focal point. Performing in a band with black and white musicians is bold enough – but a white female musician? Gayle Chapman, a young woman with strong religious beliefs, was the target of Prince's on-stage proposition – he would French-kiss her, make her perform mock fellatio, and just generally bump and grind all about her. Her tenure, however, would be a short one.

That summer of 1978, according to Pepé Willie, saw the development of what he half-jokingly, half-seriously describes as the 'Napoleon syndrome'. That is, Prince's ever-tightening grip on his players, management, assistants and anyone else who came into his contact (in our flash forwards, we will still witness this trait in him). Dez Dickerson, in *A Pop Life*, provides a light.

'He was a harsh task-master at times, but I understood that. I had led my own band before (Romeo). He would confide in me, and get information from me as to how to go about doing what he was doing. You've got to have organisation and some discipline, otherwise it's anarchy. There were times when he was a little extreme. I didn't agree with every decision he made. Certainly he was a workaholic, to say the least. But it was his prerogative – he was paying us.

'One thing about Prince is he's always pushing himself. He doesn't get complacent. If anything, he's almost neurotic about it. We were always playing, and trying different styles, and just jamming, you know? We experimented with jazz types of things and rock 'n' roll and R&B. To me that was a new

thing. It was a neat period. He had this idea that we might become a kind of black Rolling Stones. Coincidentally, this parallels exactly Kyle Bess' observations about Prince – the fact that he would be constantly recording, constantly experimenting, and always seeking out the new. When rumours were flying about Prince's decision to quit music, the engineer knew it was impossible: there was *no* way for someone who lived and breathed music the way The Boss did to *ever* give this up.

Prince's grace, character and musicianship, was not lost on the press. Stephen Holden, in *Rolling Stone* said: 'Whereas Prince's debut album stressed his instrumental virtuosity, Prince teems with hooks that echo everyone from the Temptations to Jimi Hendrix to Todd Rundgren... The simplicity of Prince's words, hooks and rhythms are pure pop. With a trace more sophistication, he could become a solo Bee Gees of the libido.'

And John Wall in *Melody Maker* had encouraging words. '*Prince* is an album of many charms, not least that it calls to mind Michael Jackson's *Off The Wall*. (From the beginning, Warner Bros. was hoping their new signing would hold much of the same appeal as the above-mentioned Jackson and then-Motown star/prodigy Stevie Wonder.) Prince's voice has that beautiful Jacksonian falsetto, and his

songs, arrangements and musicianship have the characteristic swagger of Raydio (Ray Parker Jr.'s band).'

In February of the following year, the soon to be purple one, left his management company, American Artists, for Hollywood-based

Perry Jones and Don Taylor (the latter, Bob Marley's one-time manager). This, too, was short lived when his Warner-appointed agent Steve Fargnoli directed him to Cavallo Ruffalo (who were then overseeing the careers of Earth, Wind & Fire, Little Feat and Ray Parker Jr.).

With new management behind him, he would begin a national tour in his hometown of Minneapolis on February 6, 1980. A week later he would appear in New York for the first time at the smallish 400-seat Bottom Line. Though he was selling records and the image was being fleshed out, not everyone was in awe of the act. John Rockwell, in the *New York Times*, called the show 'vulgar and derivative'. Georgia Chrisgau, in a *Village Voice* review, wrote: '"Bambi's" music forecasts what went wrong in concert. Its petrified rock and roll sound, with shrieking feedback and chomping rhythm guitar, is

one of Prince's unfortunate concessions to the fusion of rock and disco. The band brought out the clichés in the music, not the contrasts.'

And still, there were others who assailed Prince's chops as a guitarist. Charles Shaar Murray, in his ode to Jimi Hendrix, titled *Crosstown Traffic*, absolutely shreds The Boss.

'...Prince, with equal perversity (Murray has, in the previous paragraph, compared Eddie Van Halen to the late Hendrix), names Carlos Santana as his guitar guru, even as he unleashes patently Hendrix derived flourishes as both theatrical device and sound effect – though he has gone on record as suggesting that mastering 'The Star Spangled Banner' is an essential rite of passage for any tyro (novice) electric guitarist.'

During part of this tour, Prince was opening for funk king Rick James and his Stone City Band. Both artists were marrying rock and funk and a sort of synth fusion, and the pair exhibited egos as large as pregnant hippos. So it was just a matter of time before these two guitar slinging outlaws came to words – and they did. Controversy is always good and a potential fist fight is even better. Tickets flowed but no blood was spilled. James did bad-mouth Prince at every turn, telling England's *Blues and Soul*, 'He's out to lunch. Prince is a mentally disturbed young man. You can't take his music seriously. He sings songs about oral sex and incest,' and indeed he was, incorporating a new song called 'Head' in the live show.

In this time frame, 'I Wanna Be Your Lover' will be released in the U.K. and reach Number 41. Keyboardist Chapman's religious upbringing cannot find a common ground in the increasingly sexual role she plays in Prince's band, including the faking of oral sex during the performance of 'Head'. Her replacement is Lisa Coleman, daughter of Los

Previous page: **Naked from the waist up, Prince purses his lips in one of those Hendrix–meets–Jagger attitudes. He is wireless here and this would allow him even more freedom to roam about a concert stage.**

Main picture(far left): **Wearing a lace mask and laced arm warmers, he plucks on his Telecaster while another band member bows in mock reverence.**
Picture (left): **The Hendrix headband intact, Prince in a rare contemplative mood while on stage.**

Angeles studio percussionist Gary Coleman.

The guitarist has since abandoned the Gibson and now plays a Fender Telecaster almost exclusively. He will use this as his main composing instrument and in conjunction with a 16-track studio set-up in the basement of his Minneapolis home, will record his third album titled *Dirty Mind*. The album comes out on October 15, 1980 and is the first to receive any notice at all in Britain. *For You* was never released in the U.K. and *Prince* was only recognised by the black press. On this one, WEA (Warner/Elektra/Atlantic) made serious overtures to the white rock papers as well. In typical English irreverence, the press took their shots: 'Posin' 'Til Closin'' said the headline in *Sounds*, taken from a lyric by the British soul band Heatwave; and 'Someday Your Prince Will Come' chimed *Melody Maker* in June 1981.

Because *Dirty Mind* was recorded 16-track it had an edgy, rock feel to it. The guitar was almost demo-sounding, distorted and noisy, but passionate. The album, like the previous two, was essentially Prince alone; Matt Fink played synthesiser on 'Head' and the title track (which he co-wrote), and Lisa Coleman also appeared on 'Head'. Engineering credit was given to a Jamie Starr, one of the many Prince alter-egos eventually to be displayed.

This album is more guitar driven, most evident on 'Dirty Mind'. 'Partyup', 'Do It All Night' and 'Uptown' are centred on thumping bass lines, all Prince-played.

Prince and band (soon to become The Revolution) take to the road and head to the U.K. for the first time. They début at the Lyceum Ballroom in London and play before a poorly filled house. The rest of the tour is cancelled and Prince will not return for another five years. On returning home, Cymone quits the band to go solo; he sings with Prince's former company, American Artists, and will release two albums before concentrating on production.

Dirty Mind, while only selling about half that of its predecessor, nonetheless opens him up to a more crossover, rock and guitar orientated audience. Howard Bloom, a New York-based publicist hired by Prince's management, commented on the reception of *Dirty Mind*.

'The verdict from the press is clear – Prince is a rock 'n' roll artist. In fact, the press is saying clearly that Prince is the first black artist with the potential to become a major white audience superstar since Jimi Hendrix. So the task is to hold the black audience while aggressively pursuing the rock and new wave audience.'

Stephen Holden, in his *New York Times* piece, made a similar comparison. 'Prince is such a charismatic performer that his stylised salaciousness doesn't offend. With his sassy grace and precocious musicality, he is heir to the defiant rock and roll tradition of Elvis Presley, Mick Jagger and Jimi Hendrix.'

While working on material for his fourth album, to be titled *Controversy*, Prince writes – again using the pseudonym Jamie Starr – material for a new band on Warner Bros. called the Time. The Time are similar in style to the music Prince was writing circa the *Dirty Mind* period, but the more extended guitar and synth jams on the record would point more to the work which would be unveiled on the *1999* album.

Bassist Cymone – he and Prince still talk with one another, and for André's album (*AC*) The Boss gave him a track titled 'The Dance Electric' – was replaced by 18 year old Minneapolis musician Mark Brown (re-named Brown Mark). Previously, Brown played in a band of his own called Phantasy.

Prior to the release of this fourth album, the guitarist is asked to open two shows at the Los Angeles Coliseum for The Rolling Stones. Whatever hopes or illusions Prince had of becoming the *black* version of this English royalty would not find substance during this pair of concerts. Playing the bottom of a bill, which also featured the J. Geils Band and George Thorogood, Prince was pelted with rubbish and verbal abuse before fleeing the stage after only 20 minutes. This show on 9 October, 1981 was the *stronger* of the two; the one on 11 October lasted only three minutes before he was forced to leave.

Controversy appeared three days later; this album rocked and featured Prince in a new, lower vocal range (in an apparent attempt to reach a wider, whiter audience). 'Sexuality' pops with some funky chordal work; 'Do Me, Baby' is the huge, sexy ballad (which Prince had ostensibly ripped off from

Cymone); and 'Annie Christian' foreshadows the sort of synth-electro-rock which will sip up on *1999*.

Following the tour supporting the album, the singer put together another band, an all-girl trio. Originally called the Hookers, the name was changed to Vanity 6 and included Denise Matthews as lead singer (she was also a model and had appeared in some soft-core porn films under the name D.D. Winters), and Susan Moonsie and Brenda Bennett as back-up vocalists (this latter member was married to Prince's lighting director, Roy Bennett).

Vanity 6's album was recorded in the spring of 1982, at the same time Prince laid down tracks for Time's second release, *What Time Is It?*. The bulk of these sessions took place in Prince's basement studio, now updated to a 24-track machine and the precursor to the Paisley Park recording complex.

A double album, *1999*, comes out around October 1982, but it will take a full year for it to be fully realised as a musical and commercial whopper. This album, like Time's record, was recorded at Prince's new home on Lake Minnetonka, in the upper scale white community. A month earlier, the *Vanity 6* album is released and sells 500,000 copies. Again, the music on this album lets you know what to expect on *1999* – layers of synths, the Linn drum machine as main percussion sound, and even more dated organ textures recalling the likes of Blondie and the B-52s.

Due to the success of the singles, '1991' and 'Little Red Corvette', combined with a 1999 tour, the album would go gold in America by January 1983 and sell another million this same year. It has since sold well over four million units. Sales in Europe far outdistanced any of his other projects; sales outside

Picture:
Prince with wireless, shaking up the crowd with athletic and *angst*-**ridden vocals.**

the U.S. (including single and double versions of the album) were in excess of one million.

Again, Prince played most of the instruments himself, though Dickerson did provide a sweet solo on 'Little Red Corvette'. The Linn drum machine took a front seat in his music – Prince had always been a more than competent acoustic drums player, but as a programmer and rhythmic dreamer he was exceptional. Everyone from the *Los Angeles Times* to *Rolling Stone* praised the work, and even England was handing out compliments by the parcel. Tony Mitchell, *Sounds*, wrote: 'This double LP has given Prince the freedom to stretch... what has changed are the qualities of the instrumentation – now richer, more considered and much more electronic.'

Another national outing – dubbed the 'Triple Threat' tour – took place in support of the album. Prince's side projects, the Time and Vanity 6, opened the show. The tour began on 11 November, 1982 and would last until February 1983. Following the 1982 portion of the tour, Time band members Jimmy Jam and Terry Lewis flew to Los Angeles to shop some songs they had been writing. The material wasn't quite right for the Time, which was more a vehicle for Morris Day. They ultimately landed gigs producing for both Klymaxx and the S.O.S. Band, writing 'Wild Girls' and 'High Hopes' for them respectively.

The Triple Threat tour opened Prince up to audiences black and white. His guitar had become an ever larger part of the show; where he earlier used the Telecaster as little more than a prop, he would now dive into lengthy solos displaying excellent articulation, a grasp of scales both blues and rock-based, and an ever-increasing command of speed-styled licks. The tour proved such a successful crossover that *Rolling Stone* named him Critic's Artist of the Year in 1982; the *1999* album and tour and his production/composition work with the Time also garnered kudos.

But all was not cookies and cream in the kingdom – Jimmy Jam and Terry Lewis were working harder and harder on outside projects and on 25 March , 1983, near the tour's end, actually missed a show in San Antonio because they had been working with the S.O.S. Band in Atlanta. A snow storm prevented them from flying back in for the concert. Relations between Jam, Lewis and Prince would become increasingly strained.

Following the tour, Dez Dickerson would quit the group to form his own ensemble, the Modern Aires. The split was amicable, however, as Dickerson explained to another journalist.

'I didn't feel comfortable with myself any more. Because of that I became very difficult to be around. I was pretty moody. Later, I realised I was just a by-product of not being very happy with what was happening, and where we were going; and at the same time feeling there wasn't a whole lot I could do to have any impact on it. I dealt with it by being a jerk. I guess if I'd been him, I would probably have fired me.'

The Modern Aires would later appear in the *Purple Rain* film, further testament to the friendly relations these two still shared. Dickerson never released an album with his band (though Warner Bros. did sign them), and continued working as a side player for various artists including Aretha Franklin and an Atlanta band called Safe House.

Dez's absence was filled by Wendy Melvoin, a Los Angeles-based guitarist with no real professional experiences. The daughter of jazz keyboardist Michael Melvoin, Wendy had been a childhood friend of Lisa Coleman and even travelled on the 1999 tour bus.

Main picture (opposite):
The *Lovesexy* tour.

Throughout the entire tour, Prince had been pulling together ideas for a film. He, along with band members, Time and Vanity 6 began intensive acting, dance and improvisation classes. Hollywood screen and television writer William Blinn was brought on board to start sorting through a myriad of ideas. The initial draft of Blinn's script is dated 23 May, 1983 with a working title of *Dreams*. As history has since recorded it, this became *Purple Rain*, a biographical piece based loosely on Prince's own life. Also, it is no coincidence that the descriptive 'purple' is in the title; besides the fact that Prince sees in the colour a 'dark, passionate and foreboding quality', it is a homage paid to his guitar guru and mentor and his three-minute rock classic called 'Purple Haze'.

On 7 November, filming begins and will take seven weeks and cost approximately $1 million per week. On 27 July, 1984 the film would open nation-wide (four days later in the U.K.) and will take in $60 million dollars in U.S. receipts. Prince, earlier, had been holing up in Minneapolis to work on material for his next album and that would be released just a few days after the film's opening. *Purple Rain* is 'Produced, Arranged, Composed & Performed by Prince & The Revolution' and it highlights his increasingly guitar-dominated music.

In July, 'When Doves Cry' takes flight and the simple opening guitar riff combining backward tape and fuzz box is evidence of not only his own growth as a player, but also his mastery of the recording studio. The song has a breathless and timeless quality about it and the fact that it reached Number 1 in the U.S., stayed there for five weeks, and represented the biggest selling single in 1984, came as no surprise to anyone (the logical conclusion of all this studio noodling will result in his privately-owned Paisley Park facility built about a year later).

The album itself is guitar derivative and shrieks with Hendrix-like whimsy and urgency. 'When Doves Cry' is a remarkable piece of pop brilliance because, save for the opening six-string assault, there is no bass line in the song; a drum machine shoulders the tempo but everything else is stripped down, naked. The effect of this track, and eight others, was mesmerising – the album sold over one million copies in its first week of release in the U.S.

and perched itself at Number 1 for an astonishing 24 weeks; in the U.K. it was elevated to Number 7. At the 27th Annual Grammy Awards, Prince won the Best Rock Performance By A Duo or Group With Vocal and Best Album Of Original Score Written For A Motion Picture Or A Television Special (Shared with John L. Nelson and Lisa & Wendy).

Amidst this backdrop of success, however, minor problems did surface. Vanity, only weeks before the shooting for *Purple Rain* was to begin, quit the movie and the band. Patricia Kotero, a 22 year old model took her place and the group re-named Apollonia 6. Prince also began working with Sheila Escovedo, daughter of percussionist Pete Escovedo, and was instrumental in the release of her début record on 4 June, 1984 called *The Glamorous Life*.

'Music takes up every minute and every second of your time,' she told this writer. 'Everybody says it's harder to stay at the top, like Prince, but I think it's harder trying to get off the ground. It takes a lot out of you. Before I met Prince and was an opening act, it was hard. But I didn't mind it, it made you stronger. I just wish sometimes I didn't have to sleep and eat and go to the restroom so I could spend time making music.'

It cannot be over-emphasised that *Purple Rain* made the man an international commodity. Selling over ten million copies in the U.S. and a further five million copies internationally, the album *was* the first time Prince openly acknowledged the input of other band members (when crediting the project to Prince & The Revolution). In this way, he once again turned the music world upside down. By now, everyone expected him to take full responsibility for every note on a record, but by giving the nod to his fellow players, he stunned everybody. 'Let's Go Crazy' is a big, raunchy rock tune, while 'Take Me

With U', built upon a simple and lyrical acoustic guitar part, is built around Apollonia's voice. The title song rests upon Prince's guitarmanship, and from its inception 'Purple Rain' builds to become a guitar player's textbook.

'Certainly anyone who liked the Jimi Hendrix classic "Purple Haze" is a candidate for the guitar hysterics on "Purple Rain",' wrote Mark Peel in *Stereo Review*. And 'Most wonderful is the eight-minute title track, a Hendrix/Winwood-style rock ballad with a touch of cello and a hypnotic coda,' expressed *Creem* writer Jeff Nesin.

As always, Prince is involved in outside projects and on 9 July, 1984 *Ice Cream Castle*, Time's third album is released. He has written or co-written the bulk of material here and coupled with Morris Day's appearance in *Purple Rain*, the album grabs hold in the U.S. of Number 3 on black album charts and Number 24 on the pop listings. Three months later Apollonia 6 comes out and again, Nelson is responsible for all music. One track titled 'Manic Monday' is replaced at the last minute with 'Happy Birthday Mr. Christian'; this former song will become a hit for the all-girl group the Bangles in 1985.

And yet another side project was assembled called the Family, made up of remnants of the Time. Accompanying ex-Time members Paul Peterson, Jerome Benton and Jellybean Johnson, were singer Susannah Melvoin (Wendy's twin sister) and saxophone player Eric Leeds.

Another tour on behalf of the *Purple Rain* album began on 4 November, 1984 at Detroit's Joe Louis Arena. By this time, Prince was playing the 'Cloud' guitar which had been originally designed by German luthier Jerry Auerswald. This outing would last about five months, circa 7 April, 1985, where the final concert would be performed at the Orange Bowl in Miami, Florida.

Several events worth mentioning occurred during these travels. On 28 January, 1985, Prince appeared at the American Music Awards and took home three citations: Favourite Album (*Purple Rain*) in both the pop-rock and black categories, and Favourite Single ('When Doves Cry'). Prince & The Revolution actually performed 'Purple Rain' at the ceremony. But the truly noteworthy moment

happened after the gala. A select troupe of 45 artists – ranging from Bruce Springsteen and Bob Dylan to Michael Jackson, Tina Turner, Diana Ross and Lionel Richie – went *en masse* to the nearby A&M Studios to record a benefit song for Ethiopia. Titled 'We Are The World', the track would eventually become part of the *U.S.A. For Africa* album.

But Prince, for reasons only he can explain, opted not to take part in the recording, although he donated a song instead.

'They said it was cool that I gave up a song for the album,' he offers in another chronicle, 'which was the best thing. I'm strongest where I'm surrounded by people I know. It's better that I did it that way, the music, than coming down and participating there. I would probably have clammed up with so many people in the room.'

He was vilified by the press: later that evening, when the Who's Who of the recording world was down at A&M Studios, Prince and entourage were partying it up at a club on the Sunset Strip.

A little less than a month later, he played six sell out shows at the 17,000-seat Inglewood Form. Several luminaries including Elizabeth Taylor, Bruce Springsteen and Madonna were in attendance, and during the 23 February show, Springsteen and Madonna accompanied The Boss on stage for a version of 'Baby, I'm A Star' and 'Purple Rain'. The material girl whacked a tambourine and the other Boss traded licks with the purple one. In fact, it was during this performance that Prince played '4 The Tears In Your Eyes', the song he donated to the *U.S.A. For Africa* project.

Prince, as is always his wont, has been writing material during the tour, and it comes as no shock when he builds his own studio in Minneapolis to more fully develop and nurture his burgeoning ideas. Paisley Park Studios are constructed at his Minneapolis-based complex, dubbed the Warehouse, and the release of *Around The World In A Day* on 22 April, 1985 will not only be his first recording at his newly-organised digs, but his first album on his very own Paisley Park label.

The studio is originally built solely for his own use, but over the years its inhabitants will include REM, Sting, George Clinton, the Bee Gees, Paula Abdul and Tevi Campbell. In this sense Paisley Park is a combination of commercial and private project complex. From the beginning (remember that first album when he wanted no interference from outside producers) he had virtually hibernated in the studio and even when working with engineers (and other assistance) they are many times not even in his presence. So the building in his own studio, a sanctuary within which he might dwell, made sense.

There are three main separate rooms at the Minneapolis site: the newly upgraded Studio A; Studio B featuring a custom API/De Medio console; and the cozier, more intimate Studio C. These three studios sit on more than 65,000 square feet. Because this city is nowhere near as well-equipped (in terms of audio gear) as urban strongholds such as New York and Los Angeles, all of the equipment is available in-house and much of it is allowed to 'float' from room to room.

Studio A is where Prince does most of his creating. This is the mothership of the fleet and since it was remodelled within the last year or so, no other artist has been allowed to work here. A is built around a 50' x 35' main room, a large tape library and a large booth composed of granite; this, oftentimes, issued for recording drums or placing guitar

amplifiers in. The sonics here are live and bright and give a big ambient sound.

This principal room also includes two isolation booths and a huge wooden iso booth capable of housing a trio a to full orchestra. In fact, before the room was updated to Prince's specs, orchestras up to 40 and 50 pieces were recorded here.

Studio A has been nicknamed 'Starship Enterprise' because it does present an almost futuristic array of equipment including TimeLine Lynx synchronisation, surround sound capabilities, and custom-built Westlake four-way monitors. When the room was remodelled, the console was moved closer to these speakers, creating a more nearfield, in-your-face type of atmosphere.

The recorder in this SSL space is a Studer 48-track D-820 digital machine and two 24-track Studer A800 analog machines (offering the best of both formats).

Studio B is strictly an analog site and contains two Studer A-800 24-track machines and the API/De Medio console. This discrete console (there are no ICs or integrated circuits in the signal path) features custom mic preamps and other mods performed by De Medio to ensure an even 'warmer' sounding deck than stock APIs. The sound of the API is different to the SSL and allows the artist to choose from the different aural textures.

While Studios A and B are mainly used for tracking and mixing, Studio C is primarily an overdub station. This room sports a Sony JH-24 multitrack recorder and a Studer A-20 1/2" or 1/4" 2-track machine with centre code track. This entire set-up can be tied into the on-site rehearsal room. If Prince is jamming, he can roll tape via tie lines from Studio C.

As engineer Kyle Bess mentioned earlier in this chronicle, Prince will more times than not make do with the gear at hand. Though he is meticulous in his approach, he does not ruffle feathers if a specific gear choice is not available. But Paisley Park is an infinitely flexible set-up and it is rare when Prince wants something that is not there.

Tom Tucker, an engineer who worked at Paisley Park, talked to *EQ* magazine about working in the facility. 'Like most producers, Prince will mention

what he likes and what he dislikes. When I'm mixing or engineering a song with him, I'll use what suits my particular taste, and he'll tell me his opinion. There's no doubt that he is very much in charge. During the mixing stage, Prince will either come in and work with me on a track or ask that changes be made.

'For example, on 'The Most Beautiful Girl In The World' we really went out of our way to make it sound like a mid-tempo ballad. It was a marriage of old and new technology, combining live drums with sampled loops, which really give it the sound we were looking for. There were also a lot of sound effects used in the song, which helped make it visual. We wanted to use the technology to make 'The Most Beautiful Girl...' sound really romantic, and it was my job as a mixer to shape all those sounds.

'From his earliest songs on, Prince has always been very vocal about the beats that are created for each song. Designing and sampling has always been one of his fortes. Actually, he was one of the few non-alternative rock artists who was pursuing all the technology in the studio and utilising it with live players.'

Main picture (right):
In your face – the sexual animal.

Picture (above):
Shades, hair short, and a rare smile.

We flip forward once again and land back in Los Angeles, at the Record Plant, with Kyle Bess. As Tucker earlier testified, the musician was a sampling idiot savante, pushing the envelope in creating new sounds and tones. Tracks such as '1991' and 'When Doves Cry' are testament to his constant and frenzied search for that perfect missing piece. What Prince learned at Paisley Park was brought with him to the Plant, and that Anest tended to rely on several stand-by pieces of gear; the Macintosh Performer Software and the older Akai PCM-60 drum machine. But he did stray afield when the Publison, a sampler, was utilised. This unit used older technology but it provided Prince with that Music of the Spheres he was continually searching for.

'He liked it,' admits Bess about the Publison. 'That's what he wanted to use, and that's what he used. He's basically the only person I've ever used it with. It's really kind of complex to learn and use and it's hard to edit the sample on. But we used that a lot.'

The working environment was constantly changing; that is, the room and locale remained the same but the approach was always shifting and evolving. Prince was more than capable of 'getting around on an SSL' and he did need you – but he *didn't* need you. Generally, all the gear was hooked up and arranged in a common logic fashion, and then Prince would take off from there. For example, vocals were pre-bussed to tape and because he knew how to arm the console, he would simply sing a vocal part and when he wanted to shift to another track, he knew what moves to make, which cables

to plug and unplug. To this day though, what truly amazes Bess about his working method was not the technical knowledge, which was indeed formidable, but the aural landscapes he created.

'You can listen to his vocals and tell there are *so* many harmonies there. It's like, amazing, and I don't know what the secret is to that. I think it's just him singing and he prefers to sing by himself. There is something magical there – he prefers to be alone. And if I was a singer, I might too because it's an intimate thing. I guess it is uncommon because normally you have the producer sitting there, and an engineer sitting there, and sometimes an assistant engineer sitting in there, punching vocals. So the artist has to relate his idea to the producer, the producer relates it to the engineer, the engineer relates it to the assistant and the assistant is probably thinking about chicks he's gonna go bang that night. It's such a chain but with him he cuts that all out, he's doing it himself, and it works.'

If you compound this one-man army approach with the fact that Prince does his singing in the control booth as opposed to the studio proper, you are confronted with a very unique set of circumstances. Bess could not even recall working with another vocalist who cut a song in this manner but he simply muses, 'It works for him.'

Guitar-wise, Prince also worked from within the booth; his approach to guitars was simple and many times a single rhythm track provided the meat of a song (save for solos and fill tracks). The importance was in putting the idea on tape and 'going for it'. The same held true for bass parts. Every once in a while, Bess was summoned into the booth to punch in a guitar part because Prince was physically unable to play the guitar and hit the punch button. 'He'd give you a nod where to go in or out.' Prince's sound, as we mentioned on several occasions, was

Picture (opposite):
The essential Prince, naked to the world.

constructed upon one or two basic rhythm tracks and, unlike a band such as Def Leppard who stack literally hundreds of instrumental parts (that wall of sound approach), the punching in/out of guitars was not overly difficult to achieve.

Before any instruments were placed on tape, there was always the drums, a groove, the feel. Then keyboards might be layered and some sort of scratch vocal laid over the top. And then a guitar part. Again, the approach was usually a reckless disregard for convention – whatever felt right that day was the routine he followed.

This is a key mentality in trying to truly understand how this musician worked. As has already been stated, he worked with finite care in capturing the perfect vocal performance, for example, but his take may have happened at one in the afternoon or five in the morning. And he may have sung through an old tube mic or a new solid state model. There were no rules, and in fact beginning with his *1999* album and cultivated when he built his own Paisley Park studios, Prince re-wrote many statues for recording. And the sound of his records has been copied many times.

Because Kyle Bess was there next to The Boss while he was physically cutting guitars and rhythm tracks, we are able to get as close to the performer as anyone has in terms of experiencing him work. Prince is an experimenter, a constantly changing piece of the puzzle – sometimes it fits, and sometimes it doesn't. He had a somewhat slow period in the recent nineties when his music

Picture (opposite):
Still using a conventional microphone with cable, this was taken earlier on in the career.

Over leaf:
The *Purple Rain* tour with light show extraordinaire. 'Cloud' guitar is slung across his back.

left little impression; but then he revived himself with a monster hit in 'The Most Beautiful Girl In The World', and the whole world is once again holding its ears in anticipation of his next aural eclipse.

Not that this is an explanation or any answer whatsoever, but Prince has always based his grooves on mainly 8th and 16th note grooves, à la Sly and the Family Stone and that whole school. With Sly, his music was funked up by horn and guitars, and the drums tended to play mainstream rock beats: bass on beats 2 and 4. Prince has, more times than not, followed that pattern; the underlying soul and funkiness in his songs is created by guitar and percussion parts. His drum figures, in and of themselves, are *not* that funky. In fact, if you isolate the rhythm section – drums and bass – they're rather basic. The track starts breathing once he adds the percussion and samples, and usually moving rhythm guitar parts.

Recently, say within the last five years or so, many dance/pop records revolved around a triplet figure in the drums, and not a 2 and 4 feel. Prince stuck to his guns and for bad or better, was a true son. Did music, in a sense, pass him by? That's for the reader to decide.

Because he followed his own muse, Prince rarely asked for an outside opinion. From time to time, he might casually inquire of Bess what he thought about a track, but the response was never heeded too carefully.

'He never really asked me if I liked something; he only asked me if I liked a certain song. "Do you like that song?" And of course at the time I usually did. Because I understood how fast his musical abilities were… I'm not saying the song he played me was gonna be the single, but as far as the song went, sure, I thought it was cool. As far as his playing and whatever, he would never go, "Do you think that's a good vocal?".

'A lot of people *are* like that, they're really insecure about themselves in the studio and they need everybody to go, "Oh, that's great, that's great!" He never really relied on that.'

Again, we see Prince isolating himself from the outside, standing sentry at the gate to a castle no one would ever invade. Because he gave no quarter and asked for none, The Boss was able to distance himself from the people he worked with. In so doing, they tended to become less human and more mechanised; if he saw those around him in such a light, this may provide a simple insight as to *why* he treated his assistants and even musicians in such an offhanded and many times hurtful manner. In Prince's mind, unlike Shakespeare's, if he cut you you would not bleed. Bess tries to shed a light on the shadows.

'I don't know why sometimes it was easy to get along with him and sometimes it wasn't. I don't know if it was because he was having a bad day or that I was really burnt out and tired. And that's the same with Dave Friedlander and Ray Hahnfeldt (engineers). Sometimes you might get the brunt of him flipping you a lot of shit that day. Or maybe he could pick it up that you were tired and not into it. Or it could be over something very minor – he wants to run a cassette and I don't have the cassette ready to go and a level set. "Why are you making me wait? You know every night I always want to run a cassette." Sometimes it's a situation where you can't really win… you just try. And hope that you get through it.

'I'm not trying to give you the image that he's this militant, really hard guy to work for – it's just that he is demanding and he knows what he wants. I've always analysed it as he's a musical genius and it's hard to keep up with him. And I think because everything comes so easy to him, my responsibilities should come that easy to me. I guess that is his analogy, if there is an analogy there. It's just hard to keep up with him sometimes.

'You'd always try your hardest but it just depended how he was. If he wanted you to put a video tape in, you didn't want it to take too long; if he wanted you to find a sound effect out of a CD library, you needed to do that really quick. There's also a point where it's five in the morning, you've been there 18 hours, and you're going to be a little slow, you're gonna be a little tired. I guess he didn't understand that part and sometimes if you were a little slow he'd bust your ass over it. It wasn't like he was going, "You've gotta speed up, you've gotta do this, you've gotta do that." It was just the vibe he gave you. And it wasn't like I was going, "Oh, boo hoo hoo, Prince is pissed off at me," it was just this mental thing he had. It just kind of made you feel like, "Man, I must really suck at what I'm doing."'

This was one of the reasons, surmised Bess, why Prince went through assistants, engineers and musicians, like guitar strings; on the other and more compassionate side, was the simple fact that everything changes and Prince – routinely – cleaned house.

In order to secure his own seat at the round table, so to speak, Bess engaged in many non-musical endeavours. The overall term for this Princely primping was 'foofing' or 'foof the room' which,

translated in layman's jargon, means to fulfil all his needs. One aspect of this primping process was decorating the studio so it felt comfortable: the burning of candles to provide atmosphere, the

Picture (right):

A *Purple Rain* shot with lights blazing.

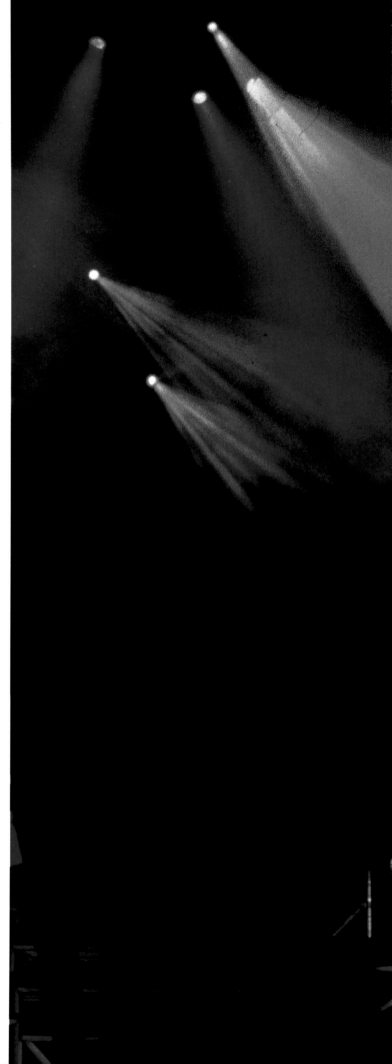

Picture (right):
A shot from the European leg of
the *Nude* tour.

burning of incense to satisfy the olfactory needs, and the placement of fresh flowers strewn about the room. Jels would be placed over the lighting fixtures to provide an ambience both softer and less clinical than typical studio lighting. Bulbs would be dimmed and the effect created was a 'nice atmosphere'. Bess admits that although he has not personally catered to the whims of an artist to an extent such as this, he reckons it is not at all uncommon. It was not out of the ordinary to have an artist want to decorate a room – whether with plants or different lighting fixtures. There was a whisper being passed about that Prince wanted the room painted – can you guess – purple. Bess, smiling, says, 'I don't think the owner would go for purple. I know his favourite colour is *not* purple!'

Main picture (left): **The Primal Prince.**

Inset picture (above): **Raving on stage.**

Over leaf: **Prince, in another Hendrix–type cap. He is constantly changing band members and in his manner takes on a classical musician's approach – that is, he writes everything, dictates exactly what is to be played, and has a concrete vision of what he wants to hear.**

The hourglass is turned upside down – this will be the last time – and we drift back to 22 April, 1985 and the release of *Around The World In A Day*. Here, in a period dominated by the Purple One, no one even bats an eye when everything around him is painted purple. The world is his, based on the tremendous success of *Purple Rain*, but his audience is taken aback when the successor to that multi-million seller bears no real resemblance.

Later in 1985, he told *Rolling Stone*, 'You know how easy it would have been to open *Around The World In A Day* with the guitar solo that's on the end of 'Let's Go Crazy'? You know how easy it would have been to just put it in a different key? That would have shut everybody up who said the album wasn't half as powerful (as *Purple Rain*). I don't want to make an album like the earlier ones.'

But he is riding a powerful wave and even though reviews were less than complimentary, it sold over three million copies in America and reached Number 1. The artist, on the road at the time, was forced to record in several different locations including Sunset Sound and Capital Records in Los Angeles, and Mobile Audio and the Warehouse (which would become Paisley Park) in Minneapolis. This is much more a collaborative effort than earlier records, the Revolution band supplying musical as well as compositional input (they're celebrated as co-writers on 'America'). This is the first record where Prince has used real strings and his début in unmasking a saxophone within his music (played by M, née Eddie Minnifield, a member of Sheila E's band). The horn appears on 'The Ladder' and 'Temptation'.

Around this time, work begins on his second film, to be titled *Under The Cherry Moon*. The first draft of the screenplay, written by Becky Johnson, is delivered to Warner Bros. executives on 1 July, 1985 and even though their reaction is less than ecstatic, they keep mouths zipped (the unbridled success of *Purple Rain* has made him a film honcho with clout).

Prior to the film's release, Sheila E's second album, *Romance 1600*, is given birth; on it, Prince plays guitar and bass and provides backing vocals ('A Love Bizarre'), plays guitar and bass ('Toy Box'), and does background singing ('Yellow'). The Family's first self-titled album comes out in September 1985, on which Prince has donated 'Nothing Compares 2 U', (this will become a mega-hit for Sinead O'Connor sometime later), and under the pseudonym Jamie Starr provides lyrics and music on every cut. The group would disband a short time later.

On 28 November, 1985, trumpet player Matt Blistan joins the Revolution, auditioning on what will become the final cut on the *Parade* album, 'Mountains'.

Four months later, Prince begins in earnest in designing the Paisley Park studio. Though he's already recorded *Around The World In A Day* there, it was not completed until some time after the album was finished. Prince has also re-designed the Revolution, adding the aforementioned Trumpeteer Blistan as well as guitarist Mike Weaver, sax player Eric Leeds, and a trio of dancer/back-up singers in Jerome Benton, Greg Brooks and Wally Safford. With the addition of Weaver on guitar, Prince is freed up to pursue a more active front-man role and in a series of dates beginning on 3 March, 1986 he exhibits exactly this. The horns now replace the musical phrases

previously performed on synth and there is a sincere jazz element present in this formation. (As an aside, in January 1986, Prince sent a song to legend Miles Davis titled 'Can I Play With U?' for possible inclusion on the trumpet player's next album, *Tutu*. Miles and keyboardist Adam Holzman added their arrangements but when The Boss heard the other material on the album, he didn't think his funk-orientated cut fit – he pulled it.)

Most of March and April are consumed with the final editing of *Under The Cherry Moon*. He also began working on new tracks with the Revolution for a proposed double album called *Dream Factory*. The material, in essence, was a return to the stripped down sparsity of the *Dirty Mind/1999* era but with modern drum sounds and patches. His non-stop work with the *Parade* album and *...Cherry Moon* resulted in the material being shelved. Several of the tracks did re-surface in different formats: one of the songs appeared on Time's *Pandemonium* album ('Data Bank') and new versions of 'We Can Funk' and 'Can't Stop This Feeling I Got' found spots on *Graffiti Bridge*. After being rejected by Minneapolis group, The Jets, 'Neon Telephone' was covered by Three O'Clock, a new Paisley Park label signing. And lastly, 'Girl Of My Dreams' was revamped for T.C. Ellis' 1991 début record.

'Parade', the soundtrack to *Under The Cherry Moon*, walks in the light on 31 March, 1986. This was yet another project recorded at the Paisley Park location (with additional work undertaken at L.A.'s Sunset Sound) and proved an intriguing blend of rock and more orchestrated numbers. Prince and second guitarist Mike Weaver trade cutting licks and interspersed with a wealth of samples and real horns, the album displays an amazing fluency.

Picture (opposite): **The New Power Generation, including Tommy Barbarella, Kirk Johnson, and behind the veil, Rosie Gaines.**

Over leaf: **In scale, glamour and style, Prince on tour was a spectacle: 'Prince is such a charasmatic performer that his stylised salaciousness doesn't offend. With his sassy grace and precocious musicality he is heir to the defiant rock and roll tradition of Elvis Presley, Mick Jagger and Jimi Hendrix.** (*New York Times*)

Many saw this as a continuation of his 'psychedelic' phase, which started with *Around The World...*

Richard Cromelin jotted down in the *Los Angeles Times* 'Apparently, Prince did not get all the flower power out of his system with last year's mind bender LP *Around The World...* because this new one kicks off with a march of toy soldiers featuring sawing strings, twittering flutes, fanfaring horns and images of "strawberry lemonade". You can almost taste the colours, man. Later, the vaguely ominous arrangement of 'I Wonder U' raises the ghost of the Beatles' 'I Am The Walrus' and the incidental instrumental 'Venus De Milo' emits a melancholy sweetness that recalls Brian Wilson's *Pet Sounds* orchestrations.'

Under The Cherry Moon opens nationwide in the U.S. on 2 July, 1986. It received almost unanimous panning, is called a flop and written off as 'pretentious', 'a mess', 'a failed experiment' and 'an ego trip of truly vintage Hollywood proportions'. Realising he had a corpse on his hands, Prince immediately re-entered the studio, Sunset Sound, and began working on music for a project with a working title of 'Dream Factory'. This became little more than a memory.

To try and revive interest in *Under The Cherry Moon*, Prince puts together details for a European tour to begin on 4 August and flies to London eight days later for the opening night. Prince sells out three shows at the Wembley Arena, and after the second show holds a post-concert party at the Kensington Roof Gardens, where he invites Eric Clapton on stage to run down a version of Norman Whitfield and Barret Strong's 'I Can't Get Next To You Babe' (first recorded by the Temptations in 1969), as well as jam on 'When You Were Mine' and 'America'. During the closing show, he calls Ron Wood and Sting up on stage to play the Rolling Stones' 'Miss You'. He will turn to Wood and say, 'This belongs to you, but when I get through it it's gonna belong to *me*.'

He plays additional dates in Holland, Belgium, Denmark, Sweden, Germany and France. The 15-date tour would be seen by 120,000 people and signalled the beginning of what the press call 'Prince's love affair with Europe'. This is highly unlikely, but...?

From Europe he flies to Japan for four shows (two at the Festival Hall in Osaka and two at the 50,000-seat Yokohama Stadium). Returning home, the ever-scrambling one starts work with an instrumental jazz-rock fusion band called Madhouse. Never able to simply sit around and slum, he starts in on a batch of funkier material to be released under the pseudonym Camille. A January 1987, release date is planned on the Warner Bros. roster but like many records, this one has the seed planted but is never delivered. One of the songs, 'Good Love', did become part of the 1988 soundtrack for the film *Bright Lights, Big City*.

Prince, always shaking up the pot, fires Bobby Z and Wendy and Lisa, and disbands the Revolution. Because of their pivotal role in *Purple Rain*, the girls will continue as a recording duo and the drummer will resume activities as a producer. Bassist Brown Mark leaves of his own volition.

In December 1986, rehearsals begin with a new band: retained are Matt Fink, Eric Leeds, Miko Weaver, Atlanta Bliss, Greg Brooks and Wally Safford; implanted are Sheila E on drums, Levi Seacer Jr. on bass and Boni Boyer on keyboards (these latter two played in Sheila E's 1986 touring band).

The following year will see the release of Madhouse's first album titled *8* and nearly four months later on 30 March, the double LP *Sign 'O' The Times* comes out. Many of the songs slated for the trio of failed projects – *Dream Factory, Crystal Ball* and the Camille album – appear here. The songs are sparsely arranged with heavy reliance on drum machine. Recorded at Sunset Sound and his home studio, the album does relatively poorly, selling a mere 1.8 million copies and only reaching Number 6 in the U.S. chart.

Picture (opposite): **The symbol or 'love' guitar. This combines all the best features of a Gibson Les Paul and the 'Cloud' guitar. There are 22 frets and a Telecaster–styled bridge (an instrument he obviously felt comfortable with).**
Over leaf: **Prince around 1986. This was the period during which he worked on the *Under the Cherry Moon* soundtrack.**

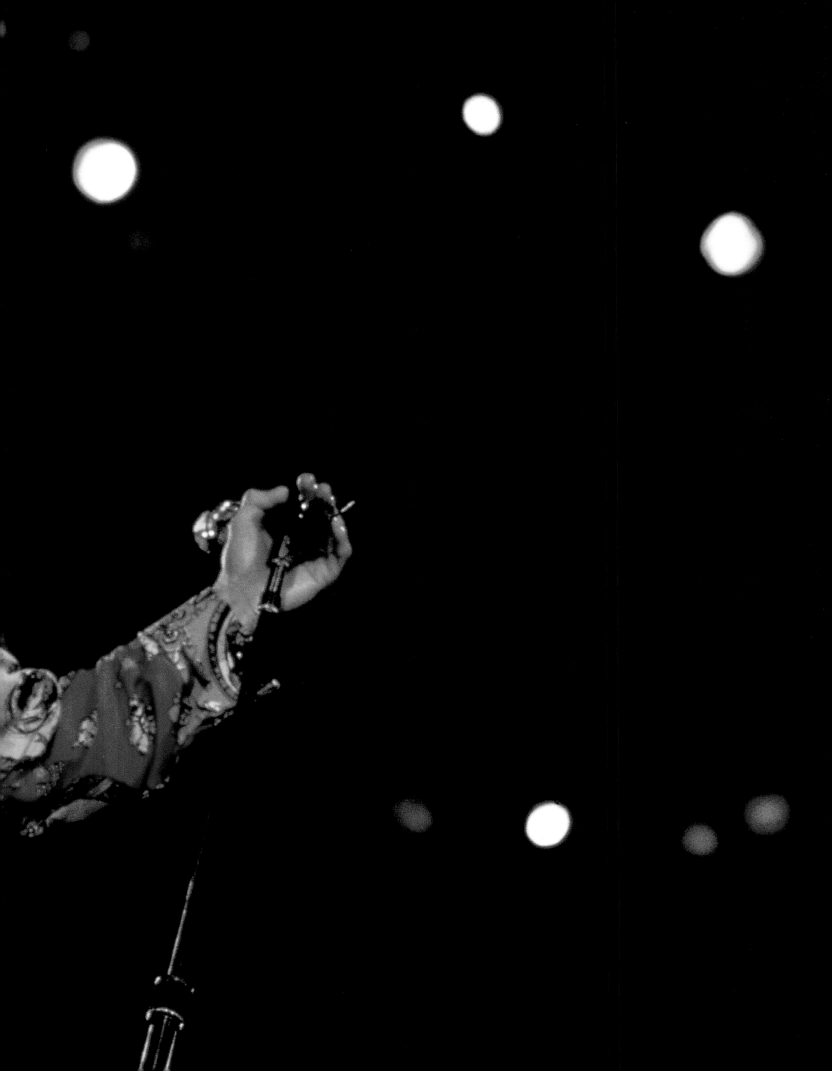

On 8 May, less than eight months after the *Parade* tour, he begins yet another European jaunt. The final date, on 29 June, at Antwerp's Sportpaleis, is a sold out 15,000-spectator extravaganza. Most of the 34 dates are sell outs and in total, 350,000 people will have gobbled up tickets (more than three times as many people who saw the previous tour).

Back in Minneapolis during July and August, he records some more tracks for what will become the *Black Album*. This is pretty much a solo album – most of the tracks were put together before any of the *Sign 'O' The Times* members were called in. The album will collect dust for several years – but this one will be released.

A film for *Sign 'O' The Times* opens in Detroit on 29 October, 1987. Filmed at Paisley Park and the final European tour dates, this one grabs the attention of the critics who hail it as a 'thoroughly rewarding film' and feel that Prince has 'never cast a stronger spell'.

Though he is riding high on the success of the

movie, he has negative feelings about the *Black Album* and consequently the move to (temporarily) shelve it.

'I was very angry a lot of the time back then,' he says in *Prince*. 'And that was reflected in that album. I suddenly realised that we can die at any moment, and we'd be judged by the last thing we left behind. I didn't want that angry, bitter thing to be the last thing. I learned from that album, but I don't want to go back.'

Prince turns to another batch of songs and on 3 December, starts hatching out the material for what will become *Lovesexy*. This one is recorded at Paisley Park with the *Sign 'O' The Times* touring band less Greg Brooks and Wally Safford. The album comes out on 10 May, 1988 and shrieks with horns and dissonance and intricately arranged pieces. In the *New York Times*, Jon Pareles said: '*Lovesexy* purveys melodies the way the *Black Album* knocks out rhythms. In fact, there's so much melody that Prince gets away with extraordinary liberties in his harmonies: long stretches of the album qualify as polytonal, with the rhythm section in one key and horns, keyboards and voices in others. While *Lovesexy* isn't as determinedly danceable as the *Black Album*, it has plenty of funky stretches. And by choosing to release *Lovesexy* after the near-appearance of the *Black Album*, Prince has let his fans glimpse the kind of choices he and other performers make routinely about image and timing.'

More touring – both in Europe and America – will run through November 1988. The year 1989 signals his split with long-time management team Cavallo, Ruffalo and Fargnoli and a signing with Purple Rain director Albert Magnoli. He also severed relations with lawyer Lee Phillips, an association

Picture (right & detail left)
Prince and his lead guitarist in an intense moment during his most recent UK tour.

which had lasted 11 years. Rumours are flying about how his Paisley Park Records label and PRN Productions are in dire financial straits and it is economic considerations that prompt these splits. But, according to one industry insider, Prince does own the publishing on all his songs, and it was revealed in the *Los Angeles Times* '...must be worth at least $15–$25 million'.

Money or not, Prince is back to work by the end of January, writing material for an upcoming *Batman* film. The release of *Batman: Motion Picture Soundtrack* flies into the night of 20 June, and sells one million copies its first week. The album really sounds more like a Prince record than a soundtrack; much of the music bases itself on simple and repetitive guitar riffs, and this is embroidered with keyboards, sampled voices, horns and strings.

About two months later, Danny Elfman, late of Oingo Boingo, would release a soundtrack of his own, *Batman: Motion Picture Score*. In a cinematic mode, Prince would begin work on *Graffiti Bridge*, his third feature film. These sessions, begun in the summer of 1989 would run through the autumn/winter period of 1989. By January 1990, work on *Graffiti Bridge* would be complete. Once again, a new band was recruited for film and live work. Standbys Levi Seacer Jr. and Mike Weaver were hold overs, while Dr. Mambo's Combo's drummer Michael Bland and three dancers and rappers called Game Boyz were hired on (Damon Dickson, Kirk Johnson and Tony Mosley). They were extras in the *Purple Rain* film. Last to join ranks was Rosie Gaines, a friend of Levi's.

It is 20 August, 1990 and Prince's twelfth album, *Graffiti Bridge*, makes its appearance. This is another double album and continues in the experimental tradition of *Lovesexy*. The music demands the listener's attention and revolves around a great deal of sampling.

Picture (opposite):
Streak of lightning or bow and arrow?

It is now 1991 and we are back in present time when Prince is working at the Record Plant with Kyle Bess. The bulk of these early songs will appear on *Diamonds And Pearls*. It is towards the end of this year, 1 October to be exact, that the album is released. A little over a year later, on 13 October, 1992, Prince will put out his 14th album, titled solely by his trademark symbol, the amalgam male/female representation. Since changing to this symbol as a stand-in for his name proper, Prince has had built a custom guitar in the exact outline of this visual moniker. In speaking with German luthier Jerry Auerswald, Prince merely instructed, 'I want it to look like my name.' Auerswald was also responsible for building the Cloud instrument.

The symbol guitar is made entirely of maple and though the jutting edges and extended filigree looks as if they might cause actual playing problems, Prince handles it with ease. The hardware is all gold-plated. There are 22 frets along this slim, easy feel neck. And in moments of panic or frustration, Prince can always use the pointed headstock as an épée.

Prince's prodigious output will continue in the coming years. A short walk down the road will see the release of *1958–1193: Come The Beautiful Experience* (which will mark his return to the highlife with the explosive single, 'The Most Beautiful Girl In The World'), the release of the *Black Album*, and the three record compilation *The Hits/The B Sides*.

Again, Prince, who might be working on several tunes at once, might start a song at the Record Plant and complete it back at his own Paisley Park amusement arcade. Bess maintains that at one point there were anywhere from 50 to 72 2" reels lying in the Plant's library, full of scratch ideas, completed tracks and simple ideas for other artists.

The engineer did develop a certain rapport with the artist and whenever Prince came into Los Angeles he would specifically request Bess's presence. Bess would try and make the atmosphere as comfortable as possible, creating a mood as we explained before, but also supplying him with lollipops (Prince has a fetish for these) and even Oil of Ulay hand lotion. Demands ranging from the abstract to the downright impossible-to-fulfil are all in a day's night's work.

'With any certain artist there are things they like. And depending on how big a star you are, people have their quirks and things they like, and don't like, in the studio. With him it was this stuff and Hall's cough drops.'

Prince would tend to block out the Plant for months at a time – that is, the main room was his 24-hours a day – and no one dared enter this domain. Bess does remember one story that pretty well sums up the Prince ethic.

'He was leaving Los Angeles, we were done, and we had the room completely broken down. I mean there was a lot of gear and a lot of stuff set up in there – the guitars, the Leslie, the digital editor, Airiq's sampling set-up, and a bunch of stuff. He got to LAX (Los Angeles International Airport) and missed his flight back to Minnesota. He calls back and wants to book another month of studio time. That's happened.'

His normal work routine was to fly into L.A. during the autumn and work there through the winter. Winters in Minnesota are akin to summers in the

Picture (opposite and over leaf):
Backlit, hands over his heart . . . the Boss.

Gobi Desert – you just don't want to be there. So coming to Hollywood for this season makes perfect sense. And when he comes to work, he does just that.

'Because he's such a creative person, we'll be doing five different things at once. He'll tell me to run over here, make a slave of this and get this groove on tape, and Dave (Friedlander) is doing editing, and we don't know what we're doing. And then all of a sudden we're working on another song while we're working on this one. It gets to be this big whirlwind of confusion in the studio and sometimes you really have to be on your toes to hang with him.'

But if we step back and try to peer through the looking glass with open eyes, it is precisely this confusion, this nebulous sort of what-is-he-going-to-do-next? aura which surrounds him that draws us to him. There is currently talk of another New

Main picture:
Pulling out every ounce of emotion within him to convey his message. Once again, the costume is different (this one is a little reminiscent of the *Sgt. Pepper's* guru jackets).

Power Generation album being released as well as a disc called *The Gold Album*. What type of music will be heard here? Your guess is as good as mine. Stories have been rife about his contractual headaches with mother label Warner Bros. Ostensibly he owes them five more albums, but in an article in *Vibe* magazine he was quoted as saying, 'The best Prince music still hasn't been released.' Gossipers say he will record under his icon symbol on a smaller label. We will see.

Prince Roger Nelson is an incredibly intriguing figure, as a self-made man, musician and miracle of morph, who is about as easy to hold on to as mercury on your fingertips. As a human being, this book has attempted to flesh him out, connect the dots of a personality who regularly eschews interviews, forbids any of his employees (and even ex-employees) from talking about him on record, and who has created in Paisley Park his own musical wonderland. All we can be certain about is the uncertain and in fact on television recently, the nameless one was once again pushed into the spotlight. Well, sort of...

Main picture:
The quintessential Prince pose? Arm behind head, arm on hip – the combination of tough guy and tender man. His is an art unto itself – if there had never been a Prince, we'd have to invent him to fill what would have been a mammoth void.

THE RECORD PLANT

The Record Plant is outfitted like a gear-head's dream and it seems worthwhile to touch on everything that was available to Prince in his recording environment. When Prince first began working at the Plant, he took up domain in Studio II; later, a new SSL room was built and that's where he would hibernate for months at a time. The Record Plant Recording Studios has provided the following rundown on each room.

STUDIO II SSL (OLD ROOM)

Studio: 14' x 22' x 12'
Control room: 30' x 23'
ISO booth: 8' x 7' x 10'
Console: 72 input SSL 4000 'G' series console and computer; 72 input SSL 40 '6' series console and control; 32 'E' EQs and 40 'G' EQs
Monitors: Custom Hidley/Kinoshita with Tad components including centre speaker and JBL 4312s mounted in surround soft film LCRS monitoring; various near field monitors, including Tannoy, KRK, Yamaha and Auratone (as will be discussed later, Prince likes it loud and rarely used these bookshelf speakers as reference)
Decks: 1 Studer A800 Mark III with Lynx Synchronizers; Ampex ATR 102 and 104s; Studer A820 1/2"; Studer/Revox cassette deck; 2 Panasonic SV3700 Pro DATs; 2 Nakamichi MR-1 cassette decks; 1 Rotel 955AX CD player; Sony PCM 3348, Mitsubishi X880 and other digital machines (available upon request/additional charge)
Microphones: Vast array of standard, rare and vintage tube mics
Video: 25" colour monitor in control room, Projection TV system in studio
In room outboard gear: 1 AMS DMX 1580 digital delay; 2 Roland SDE3000 delays; 1 TC Electronics 2290; 2 Yamaha SPX 90 II; 1 Lexicon PLM 42 delay; 2 dbx 160; 2 dbx 160X compressors; 1 dbx 165 compressor; 2 Drawmer DS201 dual gates; 1 Innovonics 201 compressor; 2 Teletronix LA 2A; 3 Urei 1176 compressors; 4 dbx 902; 1 dbx 120X boom box; 2 AMS RMX 16 digital reverbs; 1 Eventide 2016; 1 Eventide H3000 SE ultra harmoniser; 1 Lexicon 480L; 1 Lexicon PCM70; 1 Roland Dimension D; 1 Yamaha Rev 7; 1

Focusrite ISA 115HD; 1 GML 8200 EQ; 1 Lang PEQ 2; 2 Pultec EQP 1A3; 2 Pultec MEQ5; 1 Little Labs Sample Switcher; 1 Russian Dragon
Lounge: SSL II features a private lounge adjacent to the studio and control room

STUDIO I SSL SUITE

Studio: 24' x 22' x 12'
ISO booth: 11' x 14' x 12'
Console: 96 input SSL 8000 'G' Series console with Ultimation; 48 'E' EQs and 48 'G' EQs
Monitors: Custom Augspurger cabinets with Tad components including centre speaker and JBL 8330s mounted in surround soffit (or compartment) for film LCRS monitoring; various near field monitors, including Tannoy, KRK, Yamaha and Auratone
Decks: 1 Studer A800 Mark III with Lynx Synchronizers; Ampex ATR 102; 2 Panasonic SV3700 Pro DAT; 2 Nakamichi MR-1; 1 Panasonic SVHS HiFi VCR; 1 Panasonic laser disc player; Rotel 955AX CD player; Studer Revox cassette deck (on request); Sony PCM 3348, Mitsubishi X880 and other digital machines
Microphones: Vast array of standard, rare and vintage tube mics (specified microphones will be discussed in later pages)
Video: 50" Mitsubishi 5017-S and (2) Mitsubishi AM-2752 video monitors can provide a variety of displays from 'program' for mix to picture, to local cable TV programming, SSL Ultimation, Recall & Control screens as well as user's Macintosh display. Distributed house video sync is provided in each room
In room outboard gear: 2 API 525; 4 API 550a; 2 API 550B; 2 API 550b; 2 dbx 160 compressors; 3 dbx 160x; 1 dbx 165; 4 dbx 902; 1 Focusrite 115; 1 GML 8200 equalizer; 2 LA2A; 2 LA3A; 1 Lang PEQ-2; 1 Manley EQ; 3 Pultec EQP-1A; 2 Pultec MEQ-5; 3 Urei 1176; 1 Urei 1178; 1 AMX RMX 16; 1 Lexicon 480L; 1 Lexicon 200; 2 PCM 70; 1 REV 5; 1 REV 7; 1 H949; 1 H3500; 2 SPX 9011; 1 SPX 1000; 1 BBE 802; 1 dbx boom box; 1 Little Labs; 1 Russian Dragon; 1 Spacestation; 1 T.C. Electronics 1210; 1 TC Electronics 2290; 1 AMS 1580 digital delay; 1 Primetime II; 3 SDE 3000; 2 Drawmer DS 201 dual gates; 2 VP Dynamites; 4 VP Keypex II
Lounge: Studio Suite SSL I is a *self-contained* environment (this is especially important in Prince's

world of secluded sorcery and will be touched upon some pages down the road), with a luxurious private lounge featuring kitchenette and private bathroom directly accessible from the studio. Maximum privacy.

PAISLEY PARK STUDIO A

Studio name: Paisley Park Studios, Studio A
Location: Chanhassen, Minneapolis
Console: Solid State Logic SL 8088± with Ultimation
Synchronisers: TimeLine Lynx
Monitors: Westlake HR-1 four-way system; Yamaha NS-10M; Auratone and Westlake BBSM-4 reference monitors. (Prince, as we've since learned, rarely uses these shelf-top speakers.)
Recorders: Studer D 820 48-track digital machine, A-800 Mark III analog multitrack (2), and an A-820 1/2" or 1/4" analog 2-track with centre track timecode
DAT machines: Sony PCM-2500 with Apogee filters; Panasonic 3700 Otari DTR 90 TC
Outboard: Lexicon PCM-70, Prime Time II, (4) PCM-42 delays, 480L and 224XL reverbs; (2) Yamaha-SPX-900, Rev 5; (2) Eventide SP-2016; AMS DMX 15-80S delay/harmonisers; (2) RMX16 reverb; Publison Infernal Machine 90; Roland Dimension D; Jeanius Electronics Russian Dragon
Equalizers: (4) Focusrite 110; (2) Neve 31105; (2) Pulteq EQP-1A; (14) API 550A; (2) Massenburg GML-8200; (2) Avalon E55; Klark-Teknik DN360
Compressors: GML 8900 stereo; Neve 33609; (2) Summit Audio TLA-100A Urei 1178 and 1176N; (2) dbx 165a and (4) dbx 160x; (3) Teletronix LA-2A
Noise gates: (3) Drawmer DS201; (4) Kepex II; (2) dbx 904
Miscellaneous: Studer A725 compact disc player; Studer A721 cassette decks (a pair); Korg tuner

LP *For You*
WB BSK 3150   April 7, 1978

'For You'; 'In Love'; 'Soft And Wet'; 'Crazy You'; 'Just As Long As We're Together'; 'Baby'; 'My Love Is Forever'; 'So Blue'; 'I'm Yours'

45 'Soft And Wet'/'So Blue'
(no picture sleeve)
WBS-8619   June 7, 1978

45 'Just As Long As We're Together'/'In Love'
(no picture sleeve)
WBS-8713   November 21, 1978

LP *Prince*
WB BSK 3366   October 19, 1979

'I Wanna Be Your Lover'; 'Why You Wanna Treat Me So Bad?'; 'Sexy Dancer'; 'When We're Dancing Close And Slow'; 'With You'; 'Bambi'; 'Still Waiting'; 'I Feel For You'; 'It's Gonna Be Lonely'

45 'I Wanna Be Your Lover'/'My Love Is Forever'
WBS-49050   August 24, 1979

LP *DIRTY MIND*
WB BSK 3478   October 8, 1980

'Dirty Mind' (with Matt Fink); 'When You Were Mine'; 'Do It All Night'; 'Gotta Broken Heart Again'; 'Uptown'; 'Head'; 'Sister'; 'Partyup'

45 'Why You Wanna Treat Me So Bad?'/'Baby'
WBS-49178   January 23, 1980

45 'Still Waiting'/'Bambi'
WBS-49226   March 25, 1980

45 'Uptown'/'Crazy You'
WBS-49559   September 10, 1980

45 'Dirty Mind'/'When We're Dancing Close And Slow'
WBS-49638   November 26, 1980

LP *Controversy*
WB BSK 3601   October 14, 1981

'Controversy'; 'Sexuality'; 'Do Me, Baby'; 'Private Joy'; 'Ronnie, Talk To Russia'; 'Let's Work'; 'Annie Christian'; 'Jack U Off'

45 'Controversy' (edit)/'When You Were Mine'
WBS-49808   September 2, 1981

LP *1999* (double LP)
WB 23720-1   October 27, 1982

'1999'; 'Little Red Corvette'; 'Delirious'; 'Let's Pretend We're Married'; 'D.M.S.R.'; 'Automatic'; 'Something In The Water (Does Not Compute)'; 'Free'; 'Lady Cab Driver'; 'All The Critics Love U In New York'; 'International Lover'

45 'Let's Work'/'Ronnie Talk To Russia'
WBS-50002   January 6, 1982

45 'Do Me, Baby'/'Private Joy'
WBS-50002x   July 16, 1982

45 '1999'/'How Come U Don't Call Me Anymore'
(first edition no picture sleeve)
7-298883   September 24, 1982

12" Maxi-single 'Let's Work'/'Gotta Stop (Messin' About)'
WBS-50028   February 17, 1982

Two-on-one cassette *Dirty Mind/Controversy*
4-23953   August 17, 1983

CD *Controversy*
WB 3601-2   December 14, 1983

45 'Little Red Corvette'/'All The Critics Love U In New York'
7-29746   February 9, 1983

45 'Delirious'/'Horny Toad'
7-29503   August 17, 1983

45 'Let's Pretend We're Married'/'Irresistible Bitch'
7-29548   November 23, 1983

12" Maxi-single '1999'/'Little Red Corvette'
(picture disc with sticker)
0-20129   September 7, 1983

12" Maxi-single 'Let's Pretend We're Married'
(edit)/'Irresistible Bitch'
0-20170   November 16, 1983

7" Picture disc 'Little Red Corvette'/'1999'
(limited edition)
920129   1983

LP   *Purple Rain*
WB 25110-1   June 25, 1984

'Let's Go Crazy'; 'Take Me With You'; 'The Beautiful Ones'; 'Computer Blue' (with Lisa Coleman, Wendy Melvoin, John L. Nelson, Matt Fink)'; 'Darling Nikki'; 'When Doves Cry'; 'I Would Die 4 U'; 'Baby, I'm A Star'; 'Purple Rain'

45 'When Doves Cry'/'17 Days'
(available on purple vinyl)
7-29286   May 16, 1984

45 'Let's Go Crazy'/'Erotic City' (edit)
7-29216   July 18, 1984

45 'Purple Rain' (edit)/'God'
(vocal – available on purple vinyl)
7-29174   September 26, 1984

45 'I Would Die 4 U'/'Another Lonely Christmas' (edit)
7-29121   November 28, 1984

CD *Purple Rain*
7-29121x   August 6, 1984

CD *1999*
2-23720   December 17, 1984

CD *Dirty Mind*
2-3478   December 17, 1984

LP *Around The World In A Day*
Paisley Park/WB
25286-1   April 22, 1985

'Around The World In A Day' (with David Coleman, John L. Nelson); 'Paisley Park'; 'Condition Of The Heart'; 'Raspberry Beret'; 'Tambourine'; 'America' (with Lisa Coleman, Wendy Melvoin, Matt Fink, Brown Mark, Bobby Z); 'Pop Life'; 'The Ladder (with John L. Nelson)'; 'Temptation'

CD *Around The World In A Day*
Paisley Park/WB
25286-2   April 22, 1985

45 'Take Me With U'/'Baby, I'm A Star'
7-29079   January 25, 1985

45 'Raspberry Beret'/'She's Always In My Hair' (edit)
7-28972   May 15, 1985

45 'Pop Life'/'Hello' (edit)
7-28998   July 10, 1985

45 'America'/'Girl' (edit)
7-28999   October 2, 1985

7" Back-to-back single 'I Wanna Be Your Lover'/'Why You Wanna Treat Me So Bad'
GWB 0392   January, 1984

7" Back-to-back single '1999'/'Little Red Corvette'
GWB 0468   February 22, 1984

7" Back-to-back single 'Delirious'/'Let's Pretend We're Married' (edit)
GWB 0476
April, 1984

7" Back-to-back single 'When Doves Cry'/'Let's Go
Crazy'
GWB-051   August 26, 1985

7" Back-to-back single 'I Would Die 4 U'/'Take Me With
You'
GWB 0517   August 26, 1985

LP/Cassette Parade
Paisley Park/WB
25395-1   March 31, 1986

'Christopher Tracy's Parade' (with John L. Nelson);
'New Position'; 'I Wonder U'; 'Under The Cherry Moon'
(with John L. Nelson);' 'Girls And Boys'; 'Life Can Be So
Nice'; 'Venus De Milo'; 'Mountains' (with Lisa
Coleman,Wendy Melvoin); 'Do U Lie?'; 'Kiss' (later
covered by Tom
Jones); 'Anotherloverholenyohead'; 'Sometimes It Snows
In April' (with Lisa Coleman, Wendy Melvoin)

45 'Kiss'/'Love Or Money' (edit)
7-28751   February 5, 1986

45 'Mountains'/'Alexa De Paris' (edit)
7-28711   May 7, 1986

45 'Anotherloverholenyohead'/'Girls And Boys' (edit)
7-28620   July 2, 1986

CD Parade
Paisley Park/WB   May 19, 1986

7" Back-to-back single 'Purple Rain'/'Raspberry Beret'
GWB-0528   March 17, 1986

7" Back-to-back single 'Pop Life'/'America'
GWB-0529   March 17, 1986

LP/Cassette Sign 'O' The Times (double album)
Paisley Park/WB
25577-1   March 30, 1987

'Sign 'O' The Times'; 'Play In The Sunshine'; 'House-
quake'; 'The Ballad Of Dorothy Parker'; 'It'; 'Starfish
And Coffee' (with Susannah Melvoin); 'Slow Love' (with
Carole Davis); 'Hot Thing'; 'Forever In My Life'; 'U Got
The Look'; 'If I Was Your Girlfriend'; 'Strange
Relationship'; 'I Could Never Take The Place Of Your
Man'; 'The Cross'; 'It's Gonna Be A Beautiful Night'
(with Matt Fink, Eric Leeds); 'Adore'

CD Sign 'O' The Times
Paisley Park/WB
25577-2   March 30, 1987

CD For You
WB 3150-2   April 20, 1987

CD Prince
WB BSK 3366   April 20, 1987

45 'Sign 'O' The Times'/'La La La He He Hee'
(both tracks edited)
7-28399   February 18, 1987

45 'If I Was Your Girlfriend'/'Shockadelica'
(both tracks edited)
7-28334   May 6, 1987

45 'U Got the Look'/'Housequake' (edit)
7-28289   July 14, 1987

45 'I Could Never Take The Place Of Your Man'/'Hot
Thing'
(both tracks edited)
7-28288   November 3, 1987

7" Back-to-back single 'Anotherloverholenyohead'/
'Mountains'
7-21980   March 4, 1987

7" Back-to-back single 'Uptown'/'Controversy'
7-21981
April 3, 1987

7" Back-to-back single 'Sign 'O' The Times'/'You
Got the Look'
7-21938   May, 1987

LP/Cassette Lovesexy
Paisley Park/WB
25720-1   May 9, 1988

'Eye No'; 'Alphabet St'; 'Glam Slam'; 'Anna Stesia';
'Dance On'; 'Lovesexy'; 'When 2 R In Love'; 'I Wish U
Heaven'; 'Positivity'

CD Lovesexy
Paisley Park/WB
25720-2   May 9, 1988

45 'Alphabet St.' (edit part 1)/'Alphabet St.' (edit part 2)
                                       April 23, 1988

45 'Glam Slam'/'Escape' (both tracks edited)
7-27806   July 11, 1988

LP Batman
Paisley Park/WB
25720-1   June 20, 1989

'The Future'; 'Electric Chair'; 'The Arms Of Orion' (with
Sheena Easton); 'Partyman'; 'Vicki Waiting'; 'Trust';
'Lemon Crush'; 'Scandalous' (with John L. Nelson);
'Batdance'

45 'I Wish U Heaven'/'Scarlet Pussy' (edit)
7-27745   September 20, 1988

45 'Batdance' (edit)/'200 Balloons'
7-22924   June 9, 1989

45 'Partyman'/'Feel U Up' (Short Stroke)
7-22814   September 15, 1989

45 'The Arms Of Orion' (edit)/'I Love You In Me'
7-22757   October 16, 1989

45 'Thieves In The Temple'/'Thieves In The Temple Part II
7-19751   July 17, 1990

LP *Graffiti Bridge*
Paisley Park/WB
27493-1   August 20, 1990

'Can't Stop This Feeling'; 'New Power Generation'; 'Release It' (with Morris Day, Levi Seacer Jr.); 'The Question Of U'; 'Elephants And Flowers'; 'Round And Round'; 'We Can Funk' (with George Clinton); 'Joy In Repetition'; 'Love Machine' (with Morris Day, Levi Seacer Jr.); 'Tick, Tick, Bang'; 'Shake' (with Morris Day); 'Thieves in the Temple'; 'The Latest Fashion'; 'Melody Cool'; 'Still Would Stand All Time'; 'Graffiti Bridge'; 'New Power Generation (Pt II)'

45 'New Power Generation'/'New Power Generation (Part II)'
7-19525   October 23, 1990

45 'Melody Cool'/'Time Waits For No One'
December 4, 1990

45 'Shake'/'The Latest Fashion'
January 8, 1991

45 'Get Off'/'Horny Pony'
7-19225   July 29, 1991

45 'Cream'/'Horny Pony'
7-19175   September 9, 1991

CD *Diamonds And Pearls*
Paisley Park/WB
25379-2   October 1, 1991

'Thunder'; 'Daddy Pop'; 'Diamonds And Pearls'; 'Cream'; 'Strollin'; 'Willing And Able (with Levi Seacer Jr., Tony M)'; 'Get Off'; 'Walk Don't Walk'; 'Jughead (with Tony M, Kirk Johnson)'; 'Money Don't Matter 2 Night'; 'Push (with Rosie Gaines)'; 'Insatiable'; 'Live 4 Love (with Tony M)'

45 'Insatiable' (edit)/'I Love U In Me'
7-19090   November 4, 1991

45 Diamonds And Pearls/X-cerpts from the songs: 'Thunder'; 'Daddy Pop'; 'Strollin'; 'Jughead'; 'Money Don't Matter 2 Night'; 'Push'; 'Live 4 Love'
7-19083   January, 1992

45 'Money Don't Matter 2 Night'/'Call The Law'
7-19020   March 3, 1992

45 'Sexy Mf'/'Strollin'
7-18817   June 30, 1992

45 'My Name Is Prince'/'Sexy Mutha'
October, 1992

CD *Symbol album*
Paisley Park/WB   October 13, 1992

'My Name Is Prince'; 'Sexy Mf' (with Tony M, Levi Seacer Jr.); 'Love 2 The 9's'; 'The Morning Papers'; 'The Max'; 'Blue Light'; 'Eye Wanna Melt With U'; 'Sweet Baby'; 'The Continental'; 'Damn U'; 'Arrogance'; 'The Flow' (with Tony M); '7' (with Lowell Fulson, Jimmy Mc-Crackin); 'And God Created Woman'; '3 Chains O' Gold'; 'The Sacrifice of Victor'

45 '7'
January, 1993

CD *The Hits/The B Sides*
Paisley Park/WB
9 45440-2   1993

'When Doves Cry'; 'Pop Life'; 'Soft And Wet'; 'I Feel For You'; 'Why You Wanna Treat Me So Bad'; 'When You Were Mine'; 'Uptown'; 'Let's Go Crazy'; '1999'; 'I Could Never Take the Place of Your Man'; 'Nothing Compares 2 U'; 'Adore'; 'Pink Cashmere'; 'Alphabet St.'; 'Sign 'O' The Times'; 'Thieves'; 'Diamonds And Pearls'; '7'; 'Controversy'; 'Dirty Mind'; 'I Wanna Be Your Lover'; 'Head'; 'Do Me, Baby'; 'Delirious'; 'Little Red Corvette'; 'I Would Die 4 U'; 'Raspberry Beret'; 'If I Was Your Girlfriend'; 'Kiss'; 'Peach'; 'U Got The Look'; 'Sexy Mf'; 'Gett Off'; 'Cream'; 'Pope'; 'Purple Rain'; 'Hello'; '200 Balloons'; 'Escape'; 'Gotta Stop (Messin' About)'; ' Horny Toad'; 'Feel U Up'; 'Girl'; 'I Love U In Me'; 'Erotic City'; 'Shocka-delica'; 'Irresistible Bitch'; 'Scarlet Pussy'; 'La, La, La, He, He, Hee'; 'She's Always In My Hair'; '17 Days'; 'How Come U Don't Call Me Anymore'; 'Another Lonely Christmas'; 'God'; '4 Tears In Your Eyes'; 'Power Fantastic'

CD *Black Album*
WB 2-45793   1994

'Le Grind'; 'Cindy C.'; 'Dead On It'; 'When 2 R In Love'; 'Bob George'; 'Superfunkycalifragisexy'; '2 Nigs United 4 West Compton'; 'Rockhard In A Funky Place'

CD *Come: 1958–1993*
WB 9 45700-4   1994
'Come'; 'Space'; 'Pheromone'; 'Loose!'; 'Papa'; 'Race'; 'Dark'; 'Solo'; 'Letitgo'; 'Orgasm'

CD *The Beautiful Experience*
NPG Records/WB   1994
'Beautiful'; 'Staxowax'; 'Mustangmix'; 'Flutestramental';
'Sexy Staxophone And Guitar'; 'Mustang Instrumental';
'The Most Beautiful Girl In The World'

45 'Peach'
1993

45 'The Most Beautiful Girl In The World'
1994

ADDITIONAL 12" SINGLES

'Let's Work' (dance remix)/'Gotta Stoop (Messin'
About)'
WBS 50028   February 17, 1981

'1999'/'Little Red Corvette'
0-20120   September 7, 1983

'Let's Pretend We're Married'/'Irresistible Bitch'
0-20170   November 16, 1983

'When Doves Cry'/'17 Days'
0-20228   June 13, 1984

'Let's Go Crazy' (special dance mix)/'Erotic City'
0-20246   August 29, 1984

'Purple Rain'/'God'
0-20267   September 26, 1984

'I Would Die 4 U' (extended version)/'Another Lonely
Christmas'
0-20291   December 19, 1984

'Raspberry Beret' (new mix)/'She's Always in My Hair'
0-20355   June 19, 1985

'Pop Life' (fresh dance mix)/'Hello'
0-20389   July 31, 1985

'America' (extended, 21:46 version)/'Girl'
0-20389   October 2, 1985

'Kiss' (extended version/'Love Or Money'
0-20442   March 5, 1986

'Mountains' (extended version)/'Alexa De Paris'
0-20465   May 21, 1986

'Anotherloverholenyohead' (extended version/'Girls'
0-20516   July 30, 1986

'Sign 'O' The Times'/'La, La, La, He He, Hee'
0-20648   February 18, 1987

'If I Was Your Girlfriend'/'Shockadelica'
0-20697   May 13, 1987

'U Got The Look (Long Look)'/'Housequake'/'7 Minutes
McQuake'/'U Got The Look'
0-20727   July 21, 1987

'I Could Never Take The Place Of Your Man'/'Hot
Thing (extended version)'/'Hot Thing (dub version)'/'Hot
Thing' (edit)
0-20728   November 3, 1987

'Alphabet St.'/'Alphabet St. (This Is Not Music, This Is A
Trip)'
0-20930
April 23, 1988

'Glam Slam' (remix)/'Escape (Free Yo Mind From This
Ratrace)'
0-21005   July 11, 1988

'I Wish U Heaven' (Part 1, 2 & 3)/'Scarlet Pussy
0-21074

'Batdance' (the remix)/'Batdance (Vicki Vale mix)'/'200
Balloons'
0-21257

'The Purple Party Mix'/'Partyman Music Mix'/'Partyman
(the video mix)'/'Feel U Up (short stroke)'
0-21370

'The Scandalous Sex Suite (The Crime, The Passion, The
Rapture)'/'Sex'/'When 2 R In Love'
0-21422

'Thieves In The Temple (remix)'/'Thieves In The House
(mix)'/'Temple House Dub'
0-21598

'N.P.G.' (Funky Weapon remix)'/'T.C.'s Rap'/'Brother
With a Purpose'/'Gett Off'/'The Lubricated Lady'/'Love-
left, Loveright'
0-21783

'Gett Off' (extended remix)'/'Gett Off'
(housestyle)'/'Violet The Organ Grinder'/'Gett Off
(Flutestramental)'/'Gangster Glam'/'Clockin' The Jizz'
(instrumental)'
0-40138

'Cream'/'Cream (N.P.G. mix)'/'Things Have Gotta
Change (Tony M. Rap)'/'2 The Wire' (Creamy
instrumental)/'Get Some Solo'/'Do Your Dance' (KC's
remix)/'Housebangers'/'Q In Doubt'
(instrumental/'Ethereal Mix'
0-40197

CASSETTES

'Sign 'O' The Times'/ 'La, La, La, He, He, Hee'
4-20648

'If I Was Your Girlfriend'/'Shockadelica'
4-20697

'U Got The Look'/'Housequake'
4-28289

'U Got The Look (Long Look)'/'Housequake'/'7 Minutes McQuake'/'U Got The Look' (maxi-cassette)
4-20727

'I Could Never Take The Place Of Your Man'/'Hot Thing'
4-28288

'I Could Never Take The Place Of Your Man'/'Hot Thing' (extended remix)/'Hot Thing' (dub)/'Hot Thing' (edit; maxi-cassette)
4-20728   January 3, 1987

'Glam Slam'/'Escape'
4-27806

'Batdance'/'200 Balloons'
4-22924

'Partyman'/'Feel U Up' (Long Stroke)
4-22814

'The Arms Of Orion'/'I Love U In Me'
4-22757

'Scandalous'/'When 2 R In Love'
4-22824

'Thieves In The Temple'/'Thieves In The Temple Part II'
4-19751

'Thieves In The Temple' (remix)/'Thieves In The House' (mix)/'Temple House Dub' (maxi-cassette)
4-21598

'New Power Generation'/'New Power Generation (Part II)'
4-19525

'N.P.G.' (Funky Weapon remix)/'T.C.'s Rap'/'Brother With A Purpose'/'Gett Off'/'The Lubricated Lady'/'Loveleft, Loveright' (maxi-cassette)
4-21783

'Gett Off'/'Horny Pony'
4-19225

'Gett Off' (extended remix)/'Gett Off' (Housestyle)/'Violet The Organ Grinder'/'Gett Off' (Flutestramental)/'Gangster Glam'/'Clockin' The Jizz' (instrumental; maxi-cassette)
4-40138

'Cream'/'Horny Pony' 'Cream'/'Cream' (N.P.G. mix)/'Things Have Gotta Change' (Tony M. rap)/'2 The Wire' (Creamy instrumental)/'Get Some Solo'/'Do Your Dance' (K.C.'s remix)/'House-bangers'/'Q in Doubt' (instrumental)/'Ethereal Mix (maxi-cassette)
4-19175

'Insatiable' (edit)/'I Love U In Me'
4-19090

Diamonds And Pearls/X-cerpts from the songs: 'Thunder'/'Daddy Pop'/'Strollin''/'Jughead'/'Money Don't Matter 2 Night'/'Push'/'Live 4 Love'
4-19083

'Money Don't Matter 2 Night'/'Call The Law'
4-19020

'Sexy Mf'/'Strollin''

CD SINGLES

'Batdance' (the remix)/'Batdance' (Vicki Vale mix)/'200 Balloons
2-21257

'The Purple Party Mix'/'Partyman Music Mix'/'Partyman' (the video mix)/'Feel U Up' (short stroke)
2-21370

'The Scandalous Sex Suite' (The Crime, The Passion, The Rapture)/'Sex'/'When 2 R In Love'
2-21422

'Thieves In The Temple' (remix)/'Thieves In The House' (mix)/'Temple House Dub'
2-21598

'N.P.G.' (Funky Weapon Remix)/'T.C.'s Rap'/'Brother With A Purpose'/'Gett Off'/'The Lubricated Lady'/'Love-left, Loveright'
2-21783

'Gett Off' (single remix)/'Gett Off' (Housestyle)/'Violet The Organ Grinder'/'Gett Off' (Flutestramental)/'Gangster Glam'/'Clockin' The Jizz' (instrumental)/'Gett Off' (extended remix)
2-40138

U.K. (LPs)

Note: Prince's debut album, *For You*, was never officially released in the United Kingdom.

Prince
WEA K 56772   January, 1980
(See U.S. listings for individual tracks)

Dirty Mind
WEA K 39393 October, 1980

Controversy
WEA K 56950 October, 1981

1999
WEA 923720-1 October, 1982
(single LP version)
'D.M.S.R.'; 'Automatic'; 'All The Critics Love U In New York'/'International Lover' tracks omitted

Purple Rain
(available on purple vinyl)
WEA 925 110-1 June, 1984

Around The World In A Day
WEA 925 286-1 April, 1985

Parade
(available as picture disc)
WEA 925 395-1 March, 1986

Sign 'O' The Times
WEA WX88 March, 1987

Lovesexy
WEA WX164 May, 1988

Batman
WEA WX281 June, 1989

Graffiti Bridge
WEA WX 361 August, 1990

Diamonds And Pearls
WEA WX 432 October, 1991

Symbol album
WEA WX 852 October, 1992

The Hits/The B Sides
1993

Come: 1958–1993
1994

The Beautiful Experience
1994

7" SINGLES

'I Wanna Be Your Lover'/'Just As Long As We're Together'
(no picture sleeve)
K 17537 December, 1979

'Sexy Dancer'/'Bambi'
(no picture sleeve)
K 17950 April, 1980

'Do It All Night'/'Head'
(no picture sleeve)
K 17768 March 6, 1981

'Gotta Stop (Messin' About)'/'Uptown'
K 17819 May 29, 1981

'Gotta Stop (Messin' About)'/'I Wanna Be Your Lover' (edit)
K17819

'Controversy' (edit)/'When You Were Mine'
K 17866 October 9, 1981

'Let's Work'/'Ronnie, Talk To Russia'
K 17922 January 6, 1982

'1999'/'How Come U Don't Call Me Anymore' (all the initial copies with free cassettes: '1999'/'Controversy'/'Dirty Mind'/'Sexuality'/'Uptown')
W 9896 January 7, 1983

'Little Red Corvette'/'Lady Cab Driver' (edit)
W 9688 April 4, 1983

'Little Red Corvette'/'Horny Toad'
(initial copies with calendar)
W 9436 November 4, 1983

'When Doves Cry' (edit)/'17 Days'
W 9296 June 22, 1984
(Number 4 – Prince's first Top 10 UK hit)

'Purple Rain' (edit)/'God'
W 9174 September 14, 1984

'Purple Rain' (edit)/'God'
(shaped picture disc)
W 9174 September 14, 1984

'I Would Die 4 U'/'Another Lonely Christmas' (edit)
W 9121 November 23, 1984

'1999'/'Little Red Corvette'
K 1999 December 21, 1984

'Let's Go Crazy' (edit)/'Take Me With You'
K 2000 February 15, 1985

'Paisley Park'/'She's Always in my Hair' (edit)
W 9052 May 24, 1985

'Paisley Park'/'She's Always in my Hair' (edit)
(shaped picture disc)
W 9052P May 24, 1985

'Raspberry Beret'/'Hello'
W 8929 July 15, 1985

'Pop Life'/'Girl' (edit)
W 8751 February 24, 1986

'Kiss'/'Love Or Money' (edit)
(shaped picture disc)
(initial copies with stand)
W 8751P   February 24, 1986

'Mountains'/'Alexa De Paris' (edit)
W 8711   June 2, 1986

'Girls And Boys' (edit)/'Under The Cherry Moon'
W 8586   August 4, 1986

'Girls And Boys' (edit)/'Under The Cherry Moon'
(shaped picture disc)
W 8586P   August 4, 1986

'Girls And Boys' (edit)/'Under The Cherry Moon'/'She's
Always In My Hair' (edit)/'17 Days' (double pack)
W 8586F   August 4, 1986

'Anotherloverholenyohead'/'I Wanna Be Your Lover'
(edit)
W 8521   October 20 1986

'Anotherloverholenyohead'/'I Wanna Be Your Lover'
(edit: poster sleeve)
W 8521W   October 20, 1986

'Anotherloverholenyohead'/'I Wanna Be Your Lover'
(edit)/'Mountains'/'Alexa De Paris' (edit; double pack)
W 8521F   October 20, 1986

'Sign 'O' The Times' (edit)/'La, La, La, He, He, Hee'
(edit)
W 8399   March 2, 1987

'If I Was Your Girlfriend' (edit)/'Shockadelica' (edit)
W 8334   June 1, 1987

'If I Was Your Girlfriend' (edit)/'Shockadelica' (edit;
poster sleeve)
W 8334W   June 1, 1987

'If I Was Your Girlfriend' (edit)/'Shockadelica' (edit;
PVC cover, peach vinyl, with postcards and stickers)
W 8334E   June 1, 1987

'U Got the Look'/'Housequake' (edit)
W 8289   August 3, 1987

'I Could Never Take The Place of Your Man' (edit)/'Hot
Thing' (edit)
W 8288   November 23, 1987

'Alphabet St.' (edit Part 1)/'Alphabet St.' (edit Part 2;
transparent sleeve)
W 7900   April 15, 1988

'Glam Slam' (edit)/'Escape' (edit; transparent sleeve)
W 7806   July 8, 1988

'I Wish U Heaven'/'Scarlet Pussy' (edit)
W 7745   October 24, 1988

'I Wish U Heaven'/'Scarlet Pussy' (edit; poster sleeve)
W 7745W   October 24, 1988

'Batdance' (edit)/'200 Balloons'
(some copies with badge)
W 2924   June 12, 1989

'Partyman'/'Feel U Up'/ (short stroke)
W 2814   August 28, 1989

'The Arms Of Orion' (edit)/'I Love U In Me'
W 2757   November 6, 1989

'Thieves In The Temple'/'Thieves In The Temple Part II'
W 9751   July 23, 1990

'New Power Generation'/'New Power Generation' (Pt. II)
W 9525   October 29, 1990

'Gett Off' (single remix)/'Horny Pony'
W 0056   August 19, 1991

'Cream'/'Horny Pony'
W 0061   September 9, 1991

'Diamonds And Pearls'/'Q in Doubt' (instrumental)
W 0075   November, 1991

'Money Don't Matter 2 Night'/'Call The Law'
W 0091   March 16, 1992

'Sexy Mf'/'Strollin''
W 0123   July 6, 1992

'My Name Is Prince' (edit and album version)/'Sexy
Mutha'/'2 Whom It May Concern'
                                              September 28, 1992

'The Most Beautiful Girl In The World'
1994

12" SINGLES

'I Wanna Be Your Lover'/'Just As Long As We're
Together' (die-cut company sleeve)
K17537T   December, 1979

'Sexy Dancer' (long version)/'Bambi' (die-cut company
sleeve)
K17590T   April, 1980

'Do It All Night'/'Head' (die-cut company sleeve)
K17768   March, 1981

'Gotta Stop (Messin' About)'/'I Wanna Be Your
Lover'/'Head'

LV 47
'Gotta stop (Messin'About)'/'Uptown'/'Head'/
'Controversy'/'When You Were Mine'
LV 47
K17866T   October, 1981

'Let's Work' (dance remix)/'Ronnie, Talk To Russia'
K17922T   January, 1982

'1999'/'How Come U Don't Call Me Anymore'/
'D.M.S.R.'
W 9896T   January, 1983

'Little Red Corvette'/'Automatic'/'International Lover'
(initial copies with poster)
W 9688T   April, 1983

'Little Red Corvette'/'Horny Toad'/'D.M.S.R'
(initial copies with poster or calendar)
W 9436T   November, 1983

'When Doves Cry'/'17 Days'
W 9296T   June, 1984

'When Doves Cry'/'17 Days'/'1999'/'D.M.S.R.' (double
pack)
W 9296T   June, 1984

'Purple Rain'/'God' (instrumental)/'God' (vocal; initial
copies with poster)
W 9174T   September, 1984

'I Would Die 4 U'/'Another Lonely Christmas'/'Free'
W 9121T   November, 1984

'I Would Die 4 U' (extended version)/'Another Lonely
Christmas'
W 9121TE   November, 1984

'1999'/'Little Red Corvette'
K 1999T   December, 1984

'Let's Go Crazy' (extended version)/'Take Me With
U'/'Erotic City'
(initial copies with poster and sticker)
K 2000T   February, 1985

'Paisley Park'/'She's Always In My Hair' (edit)/'Paisley
Park' (remix; initial pressings included a reprise of 'She's
Always In My Hair' not listed on sleeve)
W 9052T   May, 1985

'Raspberry Beret' (extended remix)/'Hello'
W 8929T   July, 1985

'Pop Life' (extended version)/'Girl'
W 8858T   October, 1985

'Kiss' (extended version)/'Love or Money'
(initial copies with poster)

W 8751T   February, 1986
'Mountains' (extended version)/'Alexa De Paris' (10"
white vinyl)
W 8711TW   June, 1986

'Mountains' (extended version)/'Alexa De Paris'
(initial copies with poster)
W 8711T   August, 1986

'Girls And Boys'/'Under The Cherry Moon'/'Erotic City'
(initial copies with poster)
W 8586T   August, 1986

'Anotherloverholenyohead' (extended version)/'I Wanna
Be Your Lover'
W 8521T   October, 1986

'Sign 'O' The Times'/'La, La, La, He, He, Hee'
W 8399T   March, 1987

'Sign 'O' The Times'/'La, La, La, He, He, Hee' (picture
disc)
W 8399TP   March, 1987

'If I Was Your Girlfriend'/'Shockadelica'
W 8334T   June, 1987

'If I Was Your Girlfriend'/'Shockadelica'
(picture disc)
W 8334TP   June, 1987

'U Got The Look' (Long Look)/'Housequake'/'7 Minutes
McQuake'/'U Got The Look'
(picture disc)
W 8289TP   August, 1987

'I Could Never Take The Place Of Your Man'/'Hot
Thing'/(extended remix)/'Hot Thing' (edit)
W 8288T   November, 1987

'I Could Never Take The Place Of Your Man'/'Hot
Thing'/(extended remix)/'Hot Thing' (edit; picture disc)
W 8288TP   November, 1987

'Alphabet St.'/'Alphabet St.' (This Is Not Music; This Is
A Trip – transparent sleeve)
W 7900T   April, 1988

'Glam Slam' (remix)/'Escape'
(transparent sleeve)
W 7806T   July, 1988

'I Wish U Heaven' (Part 1, 2 & 3)/'Scarlet Pussy
(initial copies with poster)
W 7745T   October, 1988

'Batdance'/'200 Balloons'
W 2924T   June, 1989

'Batdance'/'200 Balloons'

(picture disc)
W 2924TP   June, 1989

'Batdance' (the remix)/'Batdance' (Vicki Vale mix)/'200
Balloons'
W 2924TX   June, 1989

'Partyman' (video mix)/'Feel U Up' (long stroke)
W 2814T   August, 1989

'Partyman' (video mix)/'Feel U Up' (long stroke; picture
disc)
W 2814TP   August, 1989

'The Purple Party Mix'/'Partyman Music Mix'/
'Partyman' (the video mix)/'Feel U Up' (short stroke)
W 2814TX   August, 1989

'The Arms Of Orion'/'I Love U In Me'/'The Arms Of
Orion' (edit)
W 2757T   November, 1989

'The Arms Of Orion'/'I Love U In Me'/'The Arms Of
Orion' (edit; picture disc)
W 2757TP   November, 1989

'Thieves In The Temple' (remix)/'Thieves In The House'
(mix)/'Temple House Dub'
W 9751T   July, 1990

'Thieves In The Temple' (remix)/'Thieves In The House'
(mix)/'Temple House Dub'
(picture disc)
W 9751TP   July, 1990

'New Power Generation'/'New Power Generation' (Pt.
II)/'Melody Cool' (extended remix)
W 9525T   October 1990

'New Power Generation'/'New Power Generation' (Pt.
II)/'Melody Cool' (extended remix; picture disc)
W 9252TP   October, 1990

'Gett Off' (Urge mix)/'Gett Off' (Thrust mix)/'Horny
Pony'
W 0056T   August, 1991

'Cream'/'Horny Pony'/'Gangster Glam'
W 0061T   September, 1991

'Diamonds And Pearls'/'Housebangers'/'Cream'/'Things
Have Gotta Change' (Tony M. rap) (N.P.G. mix)
W 0075T   November, 1991

'Money Don't Matter 2 Night'/'Push'/'Call The Law'
(picture disc)
W 0091TP   March, 1992

'Thunder'/'Violet The Organ Grinder'/'Gett Off' (Thrust
dub; picture disc)
W 0113TP

'Sexy Mf'/'Strollin''/'Daddy Pop'
W 0123T   July, 1982

CASSETTE SINGLES

'When Doves Cry'/'17 Days'/'1999'/'D.M.S.R.'
W 9296C   June, 1984

'1999'/'Uptown'/'Controversy'/'Sexy Dancer'/'D.M.S.R.'
K 1999C   December, 1984

'If I Was Your Girlfriend' (edit)/'Shockadelica' (edit)
W 8334C   June, 1987

'U Got The Look'/'Housequake' (edit)
W 8289C   August, 1987

'I Could Never Take The Place Of Your Man' (edit)/'Hot
Thing' (edit)
W 8288C   November, 1987

'Alphabet St.' (edit part 1)/'Alphabet St.' (edit Part 2)
W 7900C   April, 1988

'Batdance' (edit)/'200 Balloons'
W 2924C   June, 1989

'Partyman'/'Feel U Up'/ (short stroke)
W 2814C   August, 1989

'The Arms of Orion' (edit)/'I Love U In Me'
W 2757C   November, 1989

'Thieves In The Temple'/'Thieves In The Temple Part II'
W 9751C   July, 1990

'New Power Generation'/'New Power Generation'
(Part II)
W 9525C   October, 1990

'Gett Off' (single remix)/'Horny Pony'
W 0056C   August, 1991

'Cream'/'Horny Pony'
W 0061C   September, 1991

'Diamonds And Pearls'/'Q In Doubt' (instrumental)
W 0075C
November, 1991

'Money Don't Matter 2 Night'/'Call The Law'
W 0091C   March, 1992

'Sexy Mf'/'Strollin''
W 0123C   July, 1992

CD SINGLES

'Alphabet St.'/'Alphabet St.' (This Is Not Music; This Is A Trip - only sticker on sleeve)
W 7900CD

'Glam Slam'/'Escape'/'Glam Slam' (remix; only sticker on sleeve)
W 7806CD

'I Wish U Heaven' (Part 1 & 2)/'Scarlet Pussy'
W 7745CD

'Batdance'/'200 Balloons'
W 2924 CD

'Batdance'/'200 Balloons'
(oval-shaped Bat box)
W 2924CDX

'Partyman' (video mix)/'Feel U Up' (long stroke)
W 2814CD

'Partyman' (video mix)/'Feel U Up' (long stroke; hexagonal fold-out pack)
W 2814CDX

'The Purple Party Mix'/'Partyman Music Mix'/'Partyman' (the video mix)/'Feel U Up' (short stroke)
W 2814CDT

'The Arms Of Orion'/'I Love U In Me'/'The Arms Of Orion' (edit)
W 2757CD

'The Arms Of Orion'/'I Love U In Me'/'The Arms Of Orion' (edit; 5" box with fold-out cover)
W 2757CDX

'Thieves In The Temple' (remix)/'Thieves In The House' (mix)/'Temple House Dub'
W 975 CD

'New Power Generation'/'New Power Generation' (Pt. II)/'Melody Cool' (extended mix)
W 9525CD

'Gett Off' (single remix)/'Gett Off' (Urge single edit)
W 0056CD
'Gett Off' (Purple Pump mix)/'Horny Pony'

'Cream'/'Horny Pony'/'Gangster Glam'
W 0061CD

'Diamonds And Pearls'/'2 The Wire' (Creamy instrumental)/'Do Your Dance' (K.C.'s remix; holographic CD)
W 0075CDX

'Money Don't Matter 2 Night'/'Push'/'Call The Law' (holographic CD)

W 0091CDX

'Sexy Mf'/'Strollin''/'Daddy Pop'
W 0123CD

BACK-TO-BACK SINGLES

'When Doves Cry'/'Purple Rain'
921786-2

'Let's Go Crazy' (extended version)/'Take Me With U'
921787-2

'Little Red Corvette' (extended version)/'1999'
921784-2

'Kiss' (extended version)/'Girls and Boys'/'Under The Cherry Moon'
921788-2

'Erotic City'/'I Would Die 4 U' (extended version)
921785-2

SONGS WRITTEN FOR OTHER ARTISTS
(in alphabetical order)
(AS PRINCE)

'A Love Bizarre' (with Sheila E)
Sheila E: Romance 1600 (1985)

'All Day, All Night'
Jill Jones: Jill Jones (1987)

'Andorra' (with Eric Leeds, Levi Seacer Jr., Sheila E)
Eric Leeds: Times Squared (1991)

'Bambi (Rap)'
T.C. Ellis: True Confessions (1991)

'Bliss' (with Levi Seacer Jr.)
Kahoru Kohiruimaki: Time the Motion (1989)

'Boys Club' (with Sheila E)
Sheila E: Sheila E (1987)

'Brother With A Purpose' (with Tony Mosley)
Prince: maxi-single track (performed by Tony Mosley; 1990)

'Cape Horn'
Eric Leeds: Times Squared (1991)

'Come Home'
Mavis Staples: Time Waits For No One (1989)

'Cool' (with Dez Dickerson)
The Time: The Time (1981)

'The Dance Electric'

Andre Cymone: AC (1985)

'Don't Say U Love Me' (with Martika)
Martika: Martika's Kitchen (1991)

'The Dopamine Rush'
Eric Leeds: Times Squared (1991)

'Easy Does It' (with Eric Leeds)
Eric Leeds: Times Squared (1991)

'Eleven' (with Eric Leeds, Levi Seacer Jr., Sheila E)
Madhouse: 16 (1987)

'Eternity'
Sheena Easton: No Sound But A Heart (1987)

'Fifteen' (with Eric Leeds, Levi Seacer Jr., Sheila)
Madhouse: 16 (1987)

'Five Women'
Joe Cocker: Night Calls (1991)

'For Love'
Jill Jones: Jill Jones (1987)

'G-Spot'
Jill Jones: Jill Jones (1987)

'Get It Up'
The Time: The Time (1981)

'Girl'
The Time: The Time (1981)

'Girl 'O' My Dreams'
T.C. Ellis: True Confessions (1991)

'I Am' (with David Z, Levi Seacer Jr.)
Elisa Fiorillo: I Am (1990)

'I Don't Wanna Stop'
Red Woods: Azz Izz (1982)

'I Guess I'm Crazy'
Mavis Staples: Time Waits For No One (1989)

'If I Could Get Your Attention'
Taja Sevelle: Taja Sevelle (1987)

'If I Love U 2 Nite'
Mica Paris: Contribution (1991)

'Interesting'
Mavis Staples: Time Waits For No One (1989)

'Jaguar'
Mavis Staples: Time Waits For No One (1989)

'Koo Koo' (with Sheila E)
Sheila E: Sheila E (1987)

'The Latest Fashion'
Prince: Graffiti Bridge (1990) (performed by the Time with Prince)

'Little Rock' (with Eric Leeds)
Eric Leeds: Times Squared (1991)

'Love 89' (with Sheena Easton)
Patti LaBelle: Be Yourself (1989)

'Love Machine' (with Morris Day, Levi Seacer Jr.)
Prince: Graffiti Bridge (1990) (performed by the Time, co-lead voice by Elisa Fiorillo)

'Love On A Blue Train' (with Sheila E)
Sheila E: Sheila E (1987)

'Love Song' (with Madonna)
Madonna: Like A Prayer (1989)

'Love's No Fun'
Elisa Fiorillo: I Am (1990)

'Love... Thy Will Be Done' (with Martika)
Martika: Martika's Kitchen (1991)

'Melody Cool'
Prince: Graffiti Bridge (1990) (lead voice by Mavis Staples)

'Mia Bocca'
Jill Jones: Jill Jones (1987)

'Mind Bells' (with Levi Seacer Jr.)
Kahoru Kohiruimaki: Time the Motion (1989)

'Miss Thang'
T.C. Ellis: True Confessions (1991)

'Night Owl' (with Eric Leeds, Levi Seacer Jr., Sheila E)
Eric Leeds: Times Squared (1991)

'Nothing Compares 2 U'
The Family: The Family (1985)

'Oh, Baby'
The Time: The Time (1981)

'Once Upon A Time' (with Eric Leeds)
Eric Leeds: Times Squared (1991)

'One Day (I'm Gonna Make You Mine)' (with Sheila E)
Sheila E: Sheila E (1987)

'100 MPH'
Mazarati: Mazarati (1986)

'On The Way Up' (with David Z, Levi Seacer Jr., Elisa Fiorillo)
Elisa Fiorillo: I Am (1990)

'Ooh This Need'
Elisa Fiorillo: I Am (1990)

'Overnight, Every Night' (with Eric Leeds, Levi Seacer Jr., Sheila E)
Eric Leeds: Times Squared (1991)

'Playgirl'
Elisa Fiorillo: I Am (1990)

'Pride And The Passion' (with Sheila E)
Sheila E: Sheila E (1987)

'Qualified' (with Kirk Johnson)
Lois Lane: Precious (1992)

'Release It' (with Morris Day. Levi Seacer Jr.)
Prince: Graffiti Bridge (1990) (performed by the Time)

'Round And Round'
Prince: Graffiti Bridge (1990) (lead voice by Tevin Campbell)

'The Sex Of It'
Kid Creole and the Coconuts: Private Waters in the Great Divide (1990)

'Shake!' (with Morris Day)
Prince: Graffiti Bridge (1990) (performed by the Time)

'Shall We Dance'
Brownmark: Good Feeling (1989)

'Sixteen' (with Eric Leeds)
Madhouse: 16 (1987)

'So Strong'
Dale: Riot in English (1988)

'Spirit' (with Levi Seacer Jr., Martika, Frankie Blue)
Martika: Martika's Kitchen (1991)

'Stand Back' (with Stevie Nicks)
Stevie Nicks: The Wild Heart (1983)

'The Stick'
The Time: The Time (1981)

'Sticky Wicked'
Chaka Khan: CK (1988)

'T.C.'s Rap' (with T.C. Ellis)
Prince: maxi-single track (1990) (performed by T.C. Ellis)

'Ten And *******' (with Eric Leeds, Levi Seacer Jr., Sheila E)
Madhouse: Single B-side (1987)

'Thirteen and *******' (with Eric Leeds, Levi Seacer Jr., Sheila E)
Madhouse: Single B side (1987)

'Time Waits For No One' (with Mavis Staples)
Mavis Staples: Time Waits For No One (1989)

'Times Squared' (with Eric Leeds)
Eric Leeds: Times Squared (1991)

'Train'
Mavis Staples: Time Waits For No One (1989)

'With This Tear'
Celine Dion: Celine Dion (1992)

'Wouldn't You Love To Love Me?'
Taja Sevelle: Taja Sevelle (1987)

'Yo Mister'
Patti LaBelle: Be Yourself (1989)

AS JAMIE STARR

'A Million Miles (I Love You)' (with Lisa Coleman)
Apollonia 6: Apollonia 6 (1984)

'The Belle If St. Mark'
Sheila E: The Glamorous Life (1984)

'The Bird' (with Morris Day, Jesse Johnson)
The Time: Ice Cream Castle (1984)

'Bite The Beat' (with Jesse Johnson)
Vanity 6: Vanity 6 (1982)

'Blue Limousine'
Apollonia 6: Apollonia 6 (1984)

'Chili Sauce' (with Morris Day, Paul Peterson)
The Time: Ice Cream Castle (1984)

'Chocolate'
The Time: Pandemonium (1990)

'Data Bank'
The Time: Pandemonium (1990)

'Desire'
The Family: The Family (1985)

'Donald Trump (Black version)'
The Time: Pandemonium (1990)

'Drive Me Wild'
Vanity 6: Vanity 6 (1982)

'Gigolos Get Lonely Too'
The Time: What Time Is It? (1982)

'The Glamorous Life'
Sheila E: The Glamorous Life (1984)

'Grace'
The Time: Single B side (1982)

'Happy Birthday Mr. Christian'
Apollonia 6: Apollonia 6 (1984)

'High Fashion'
The Family: The Family (1985)

'I Don't Wanna Leave You'
The Time: What Time Is It? (1982)

'Ice Cream Castles' (with Morris Day, Jesse Johnson)
The Time: Ice Cream Castle (1984)

'If A Girl Answers (Don't Hang Up)' (with Terri Lewis)
Vanity 6: Vanity 6 (1982)

'If The Kid Can't Make You Come' (with Morris Day, Jesse Johnson)
The Time: Ice Cream Castle (1984)

'In A Spanish Villa'
Apollonia 6: Apollonia 6 (1984)

'Jerk Out' (with Morris Day, Jimmy Jam, Terry Lewis)
The Time: Pandemonium (1990)

'Jungle Love' (with Morris Day)
The Time: Pandemonium (1990)

'Make Up'
Vanity 6: Vanity 6 (1982)

'Mutiny'
The Family: The Family (1985)

'My Drawers' (with Morris Day, Jesse Johnson)
The Time: Ice Cream Castle (1984)

'My Summertime Thang'
The Time: Pandemonium (1990)

'Nasty Girl'
Vanity 6: Vanity 6 (1982)

'Next Time Wipe The Lipstick Off Your Collar'
Sheila E: The Glamorous Life (1984)

'Noon Rendezvous' (with Sheila E)
Sheila E: The Glamorous Life (1984)

'Oliver House'
Sheila E: The Glamorous Life (1984)

'Onedayi'mgonnabesomebody'
The Time: What Time Is It? (1982)

'Ooh She She Wa Wa'
Apollonia 6: Apollonia 6 (1984)

'The Screams Of Passion'

The Family: The Family (1985)

'777–9311'
The Time: What Time Is It? (1982)

'Sex Shooter'
Apollonia 6: Apollonia 6 (1984)

'Shortberry Strawcake'
Sheila E: The Glamorous Life (1984)

'Some Kind Of Lover' (with Brenda Bennett)
Apollonia 6: Apollonia 6 (1984)

'Susannah's Pajamas' (with Eric Leeds)
The Family: The Family (1985)

'3 x 2 = 6'
Vanity 6: Vanity 6 (1982)

'Tricky'
The Time: Single B side (1984)

'The Walk'
The Time: What Time Is It? (1982)

'Wet Dream'
Vanity 6: Vanity 6 (1982)

'Wild And Loose' (with Dez Dickerson)
The Time: What Time Is It? (1982)

'Yes' (with Eric Leeds)
The Family: The Family (1985)

AS MADHOUSE

'One'
Madhouse: 8 (1987)

'Two'
Madhouse: 8 (1987)

'Three'
Madhouse: 8 (1987)

'Four'
Madhouse: 8 (1987)

'Five'
Madhouse: 8 (1987)

'Six'
Madhouse: 8 (1987)

'Seven'
Madhouse: 8 (1987)

'Eight'
Madhouse: 8 (1987)

'Nine'
Madhouse: 8 (1987)

'Twelve'
Madhouse: 8 (1987)

'Thirteen'
Madhouse: 8 (1987)

'Fourteen'
Madhouse: 8 (1987)

AS JOEY COCO

'Baby Go-Go'
Nona Hendryx: Female Trouble (1987)

'Baby, You're A Trip'
Jill Jones: Jill Jones (1987)

'Cool Love'
Sheena Easton: The Lover In Me (1988)

'My Man'
Jill Jones: Jill Jones (1987)

'Neon Telephone'
Three O'Clock: Vermillion (1988)

'101'
Sheena Easton: The Lover In Me (1988)

'Telepathy'
Deborah Allen: Telepathy (1987)

'Violet Blue'
Jill Jones: Jill Jones (1987)

'You're My Love'
Kenny Rogers: They Don't Make Them Like They Used To (1987)

AS ALEXANDER NEVERMIND

'Sugar Walls'
Sheena Easton: A Private Heaven (1984)

AS PAISLEY PARK

'Elephant Box' (with Ingrid Chavez)
Ingrid Chavez: Chavez: May 19, 1992 (1991)

'Heaven Must Be Near' (with Levi Seacer Jr., Ingrid Chavez)
Ingrid Chavez: Chavez: May 19, 1992 (1991)

'I Hear Your Voice' (with Rosie Gaines, Francis Jules)

Patti LaBelle: Burnin' (1991)

'Jadestone' (with Ingrid Chavez)
Ingrid Chavez: Chavez: May 19, 1992 (1991)

'Slappy Dappy' (with Ingrid Chavez)
Ingrid Chavez: Chavez: May 19, 1992 (1991)

'Tip 'O' My tongue' (with Kirk Johnson)
El DeBarge: In The Storm (1992)

'U'
Paula Abdul: Spellbound (1991)

'Whispering Dandelions' (with Ingrid Chavez)
Ingrid Chavez: Chavez: May 19, 1992 (1991)

AS CHRISTOPHER TRACY

'Manic Monday'
The Bangles: Different Light (1986)

BOOTLEGS

1 *A Beautiful Night*; source = Westalenhalle, Dortmund, June 2, 1987; quality = VG; format = double LP
2 *A Love Bizarre*; source = *Sign 'O' The Times* film; quality = EX; format = double LP
3 *The Back Album*; source = official releases; quality = EX; format = LP
4 *Black Album/Crystal Ball*; source = *Black Album* and studio outtakes from 1986; quality = *Black Album* tracks are EX, others range form VG to EX; format = CD. Contains a booklet with lyrics to *Black Album*. Two releases exist and only difference is difference in quality of paper
5 *Charade*; source = studio outtakes circa 1985–86; quality = EX; format = LP and CD. There are three LP releases all with same cover but different labels; Planet Rock Records, B&W Records, and Paisley Park. This latter version is limited release with only 500 known copies
6 *Crucial*; source = studio outtakes circa 1986–87; quality = VG+ to EX; format = CD and LP. There are at least three different releases in CD format, all with different covers; two LP releases with individual covers
7 *I Wanna Be Your Lover, Miss B*; source = Waldstation, Frankfurt, August 27, 1988; quality = VG; format = double LP
8 *Japan*; source = Rainbow Hall, Nagoya, February 8, 1989; quality = VG; format = double LP.
9 *Live 4 Love*; source = Alsterdorfer Sporthalle, Hamburg, June 9, 1990; quality = VG; format = multiple LP set
10 *Nude Tour 1990*; source = Wembley Arena, June 19, 1990; quality = VG; format = triple LP
11 *The Red Album*; source = Minnesota Music Awards, Carlton Celebrity Room, Minneapolis, May 20, 1986; quality = VG to VG+; format = CD

12 *Royal Jewels*; source = Studio outtakes 1983–86; quality = VG to EX; format = triple LP box set
13 *Sign 'O' The Times Tour 1987*; source = Palatrussardi, Milan, June 9, 1987; quality = VG; format = double LP (two releases on different labels, same covers)
14 *Super Funks*; source = New Orleans, February 25, 1982; quality = EX to VG; format = CD
15 *Uncut Diamonds*; source = Studio outtakes 1990–91; quality = EX; format = CD
16 *Wonderboy*; source = Palais Omnisport, Paris, June, 1987; quality = VG to EX; format = double CD

*Rating chart: EX = excellent; VG = very good; G = good; F =fair; and P = poor

* Prince is bootlegged like few other artists in history. This is meant only as a random sampling as an indication of what is available (if you look hard enough)